CHALFORD
Oral History
SERIES

MACHEN
remembered

'Machen Remembered' came into existence in January 1995 with the aim of compiling an archive of the changes that had occurred during the lifetime of many of the older members of the village. The need to pass on the memories of events and people who helped to shape what we are today, is what this book is about. We have also been told that the therapy of so doing is 'better than any medicine'. Our logo is the 'conker tree' which stood at the heart of the village. Like so many other things it too has gone, but it has not been forgotten. We have endeavoured to turn back the clock 100 years from the middle of this century, and to pick out the most salient points from the ever increasing wealth of material that has been made available to us. To those who have supplied reminiscences, which due to limitations of space we have been unable to use in this book, we offer our thanks and apologies. Rest assured that they have been recorded and stored in our archive for future use. Welsh spellings have been adopted except for the commonly used form of VEDW.

CHALFORD
Oral History
SERIES

MACHEN
remembered

Compiled by
Eric & Delphine Coleman, Dennis Spargo
and fellow members of Machen Remembered

CHALFORD

First published 1996
Copyright © Eric & Delphine Coleman, Dennis Spargo
and fellow members of Machen Remembered, 1996

The Chalford Publishing Company
St Mary's Mill, Chalford,
Stroud, Gloucestershire, GL6 8NX

ISBN 0 7524 0737 6

Typesetting and origination by
The Chalford Publishing Company
Printed in Great Britain by
Redwood Books, Trowbridge

Front cover and illustration below:

Unemployed Machen miners, from Nine Mile Point colliery, who were given temporary employment building the new Cardiff Road during the Miners' Strike of 1926. The group includes: Matt Bennett, David Evans, George Rogers, George Burton, Alfred Davies, Bob Escott, Major Vincent (in charge), George Harrington, Len Wollan, Victor Whittingham, George Kellow, Jim Griffiths, Jack Willetts and Ted Buckley.

The old post office and Ffwrrwm Ishta, c. 1900.

Contents

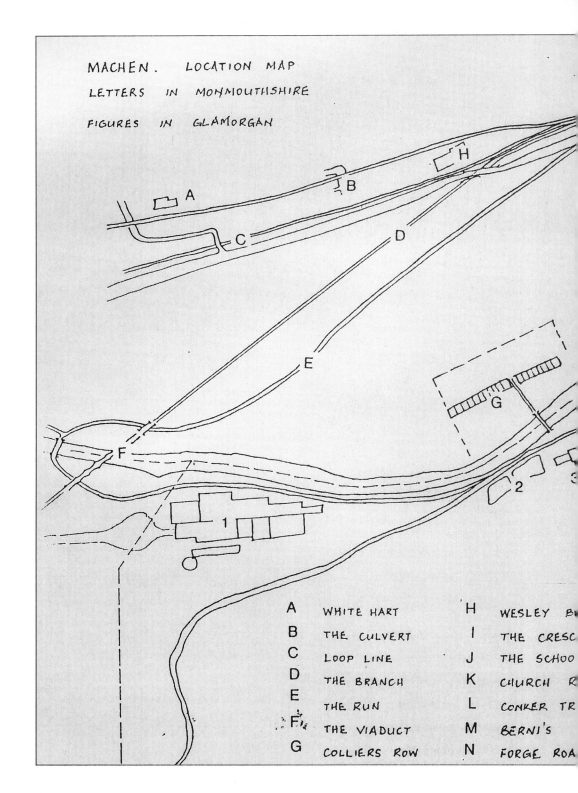

MACHEN. LOCATION MAP
LETTERS IN MONMOUTHSHIRE
FIGURES IN GLAMORGAN

A	WHITE HART	H	WESLEY B...
B	THE CULVERT	I	THE CRESC...
C	LOOP LINE	J	THE SCHOO...
D	THE BRANCH	K	CHURCH R...
E	THE RUN	L	CONKER TR...
F	THE VIADUCT	M	BERNI'S
G	COLLIERS ROW	N	FORGE ROA...

6

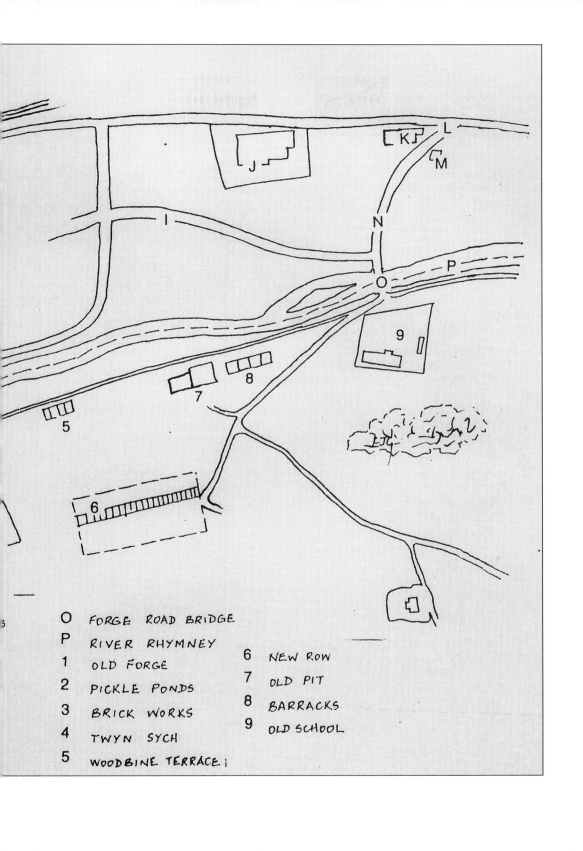

O   FORGE ROAD BRIDGE
P   RIVER RHYMNEY
1   OLD FORGE   6   NEW ROW
2   PICKLE PONDS   7   OLD PIT
3   BRICK WORKS   8   BARRACKS
4   TWYN SYCH   9   OLD SCHOOL
5   WOODBINE TERRACE

Foreword

By Mr Ron Davies MP (Caerphilly) and Shadow Secretary of State for Wales

It gives me great pleasure to have been asked to write a foreword to Machen Remembered. Three generations of my family have lived in Machen, and I was born in the village just after the Second World War. My formative years were spent in and around the countryside and farms of Machen. I was educated in the local school which, at that time, had separate infant and junior schools, and where, amongst the other teachers, Mr Spinks, Miss Mayberry and Mrs Harrington left lasting impressions. My mother taught in the infant school for many years until her retirement in 1972, and the headteacher at that time was Miss Hopkins. Although, nowadays, I spend most of my working time in London I look forward to returning home to the peace and tranquillity of Machen and the surrounding countryside.

Machen has seen many changes, some of which include occupation by the Romans – visible by the lead mine remains. Charcoal burners brought with them the destruction of much of the woodland surrounding the village. During the early part of this century Machen was quite an industrialised area, with the local foundry, the tinworks and the coal mine bringing much employment not only to local people, but also for outsiders who came to seek work and eventually settled in the village. The three railway lines were a major factor in the prosperity of Machen – the Newport to Brecon line carried goods, and goods/passenger lines ran from Newport to Caerphilly. Later, during the years of the Second World War, Machen proved to be a safe haven for many children who were evacuated from vulnerable cities such as London to live in the safe confines of the village.

Nowadays Cray Valley and ARC Machen Quarry (which still uses a railway line to Newport) are the major employers. Much of Machen remains agricultural, and people move to the village to live in a rural community which has good communication links to places of employment.

Many of the old, well-served chapels have long been demolished, some to make way for housing development. Indeed new housing development is currently changing the face of Machen. It is, therefore, important that the valuable work being carried out by Machen Remembered should be recorded for posterity in order to reflect such changes not only for the present, but also for future generations interested in the life of their ancestors and the development of Machen. I would like to thank the Committee of Machen Remembered for their enthusiasm in undertaking to produce such a publication which, I have no doubt, will be of much interest and enjoyment to all who have the opportunity to read it.

Machen
Summer 1996

One
Industry

Machen's ancient industrial heritage stems back to Roman lead mining at Cefn Pwll Du near Draethen. Coal mining in Machen Forest is recorded in 1316, and charcoal burning contributed revenue of £215 in 1403 to the Exchequer. This lucrative source was curtailed when the local inhabitants rose in support of Owain Glyn Dŵr! Iron was being forged at Rhyd-y-gwern by Corslett Tinkhaus from Germany in 1567, and Machen forge was in existence by 1569. By 1680 horses and mules were hauling pig iron from the Van furnaces in Caerphilly to two forges situated at Machen and Gelliwastad where it would be converted to the different grades produced there, including the malleable Osmund iron used in the production of wire. The Tredegar Estate archives give detailed accounts of coal miners, coal carriers and lime carriers working at Machen in 1684, together with details of iron and tin pipes lying in Machen Lead Mine a century later in 1784.

Charcoal burners at work in Machen, 1960. At one time charcoal was produced for sale in small packets as a remedy for digestive complaints.

Gelliwastad (the level grove), the first recorded mention of which dates from 1447 in the Account of Ieuan ap David ap Howell, Receiver of Machen Forest. In 1465 a payment of 6s 8d was made to the Machen beadle for the custody of a hawk's nest in the forest of Gelliwastad – known to locals simply as 'the Gelli'.

Machen forge

Machen forge continued to process iron until the early 1820s, demand during the late eighteenth and early nineteenth century having been high during the Napoleonic Wars. It was at this time, c. 1826, that the forge was enlarged and adapted by William and Joseph Russell to enable the manufacture of tin-plate to be undertaken in addition to the forging of iron. Joseph Russell was then living at Gelliwastad, which had been the residence of several earlier forge managers.

The demand for tin-plate was occasioned by the growth of the canning industry which was pioneered in France. By 1812 food was being preserved in tinned iron containers for the forces, but it was not generally accepted by the civilian population here until the mid-nineteenth century. America, however, was using vast quantities of tin-plate for canning food and the production of petrol containers, and by 1873 Machen forge was producing 40,000 boxes of tin-plate a year, much of it for export to the USA.

The 1841 census records a Philip Woodruff living with his wife and young family at Bovil House, his occupation being given as an iron and tin-plate manufacturer. He became a partner of the Russells in the 1850s, and at the time of the 1871 census he was the sole proprietor of the Machen Iron and Tinplate Works, which was then employing 200 men and 130 boys and girls.

These industries which had led to the growth of Upper Machen in the mid-1800s, were in decline by the beginning of the twentieth century.

Machen Iron and Tin Works, c. 1850 (image courtesy of the Welsh Industrial and Maritime Museum). A recession in the tin-plate industry, together with failure to update machinery, caused the closure of the Machen Iron and Tin Works in 1887, although the Waterloo Iron and Tinplate Company in Rudry parish, which had started trading in 1876, continued in production.

Soup kitchen of 1887

The impact of the closure of Machen Iron and Tin Works on the village work force must have been disastrous. The diaries of Philip Woodruff record that a soup kitchen was opened at the Ffwrrwm Ishta in January 1887, and coal from Risca colliery was distributed to those in need. He also noted the cost to the ratepayers, who also had to pay towards the running of the schools.

'First boiling of soup, 40 lbs. meat, carrots, onions, £1. 2. 9. Made 40 gallons of excellent soup. About 60 gallons of soup given away, finished peas given by I.R. Jacob. Poor Rate very heavy £365. 0. 0. this with School Board of £248 will make about 2/6d. in the £, very heavy indeed.' [Diary of PW]

Traces of the forge today

Today there is little evidence to any stranger that the forge-cum-tinworks ever existed. The name Forge Road is one indicator, and if you walk alongside Green Lane and the river to the footbridge, adjacent to the forge site and the viaduct, you can see traces of foundation walls and the brickwork opening where a water-wheel was placed with the leat (water channel) close by to work the forge-hammers. Over the bridge there are traces of sidings near the river where drams would be parked ready for the journey up the dram road ('the Run') to Upper Machen and the Rumney Tramroad, and thence onward to Newport Docks and destinations such as Bristol. The 1881 census shows the many varied occupations carried out by the work force. These included: plate doublers, picklers, annealers, shinglers, tin-plate openers, hammer men, bran girls, bran rubbers, tin-plate scourers, tin-plate dippers, refiners and stokers.

William Hicks, forgeman and bar roller (died 1914, aged 95). For nearly 150 years members of the Hicks family worked at Machen forge, from William Hicks born 1719 in Herefordshire to James Hicks who was still working there at the age of 79 in 1871. Philip Woodruff mentions another worker, Samuel Winmill, whose family, in common with the Hickses, have descendants today in Machen. In the 1880s, some members of the Hicks family emigrated to America where they took up similar employment in the expanding US tin-plate industry.

Two forgemen

'My grandfather told me that his father, William, who died in 1914 aged 95, worked at the old charcoal forge in the last century. He said that when a number of workmen were digging foundations there in 1860, they found masses of iron cinders from ancient blast furnaces which nobody knew about.' [JH]

'Old Sam Winmill buried today about 82 years. I believe he was one of the first that came to Machen Tin Works about the year 1840, and has not left the place since, but he has now gone to his last resting place for ever.' [Diary of PW, 1893. He died at the age of 79 and his grave is in St John's graveyard]

The forge this century

There was little activity at the forge after its demise in 1887, although during the First World War (1914-1918), a local paper reported that women navvies were employed to remove heaps of iron slag from dumps remaining on the site which were considered worth salvaging for munitions.

By 1920 many of the buildings had gone, but repairs to Tredegar Estate property on the Glamorgan side of the river in the early part of this century were dealt with from a base on the old forge site which was Tredegar land. The accounts of Thomas Jones, the blacksmith at Lower Machen, record that he was regularly supplying gates, hasps, chains and bolts to Machen forge and shop. On one occasion he billed £2. 5s 0d for iron work on a footbridge at Machen forge shop, sometimes called the Carpenter's Shop. These accounts were sent to Lord Tredegar, Glamorgan Estate.

Forge Cottage, one-time home of the Haskins family, destroyed by fire. It was adjacent to Machen forge, viaduct and footbridge.

Machen Forge Engineering Works

In 1920 a small engineering plant known as Machen Forge Engineering Works was operating in the buildings that remained. This small business had contracts with the Brecon and Merthyr Railway for repair of rolling stock, but when the B. & M. amalgamated with the Great Western Railway (GWR), this was to prove disastrous. The GWR also had repair shops at Caerphilly and decided to do all the work themselves. Consequently, this small business had to close down in 1924.

'My father, Charlie Rogers, set this up, and working with him were Horace Jones, Bert Adams and Ivor Sainsbury. I was only a little lad then, but I can vividly picture the open furnace at one end of the building, benches and anvils, and an overhead hand-chain type of gantry to carry the heavier articles into position. We boys would stand around and watch my father doing the acetylene welding. It was also a playground for us because there was an old steam traction engine standing on the site; it was not in use, but we had great fun clambering all over it, and in our imagination, driving it. A few years before, the bridge at Colliers Row nearby had collapsed, but the men put some wood planks across the river a little lower down so that they could take the short cut to their work. The local boys would often take dares to walk across blindfold. My memories as a child of six years of the old Machen Forge Engineering Works are quite happy and, indeed, very vivid.' [AR]

Bricks found on the old site of the Machen Brick, Stone, Lime and Coal Company between Green Row and the forge which closed down probably early this century. It produced one million bricks a year, mostly yellow, many of which can be seen inserted round windows and doors in the older Machen houses. There are still traces of brick ash to be seen on this site, together with one remaining wall. Many loads of rubble were transported from the site in the 1950s to provide foundations for the Llanwern Steel Works. There was a second brickworks near Bovil House, which in 1864 was run by John Brewer and Son, who also worked the Bovil farm.

'I would go with my Uncle Tom to collect the old broken bricks and ash to make paths in our garden, this would be about sixty-five years ago.' [EJC]

'There used to be an old chap there, George Greenhaf, but everyone called him 'George Nunc', and when the kilns were alight he would let us take our potatoes over there, and put them under the ashes.' [LR]

One of the many man-hole covers to be found in Machen, an abiding epitaph to Machen Foundry.

Machen Foundry

This was another concern initially owned by Russell and Woodruff and later solely by the Woodruff family. They were iron and brass founders, boiler makers, and manufacturers of railway wheels and waggons. The foundry was adjacent to Machen railway station, and had a furnace for tyre-making, a truck-making branch and an engineering shop which manufactured building sundries and smithing tools. At the end of the 1800s its workforce numbered forty or so men, comprising fitters, carpenters, masons, moulders, dressers and labourers. Chairs (iron sockets with a deep groove designed to take a railway rail which was secured to sleepers) were made for the Alexandra Newport Docks & Railway Co. Ltd. An old Foundry wages book shows one moulder, John Watkins, was paid 5/6d a ton for this job, and in one month he made a total of 3,978 chairs weighing 46 tons which earned him £12. 17s 9d. Carpenters making trucks using oak and elm were paid £3 a truck. Originally, the foundry worked

These beautifully fashioned iron gates at the entrance to Bovil House, the one time home of the Woodruffs, and lastly of Sir Alfred and Lady Nicholas, were made in Machen foundry.

for the Rumney tramroad, but with the growth of the Brecon and Merthyr Railway and their amalgamation with the GWR in 1923, it declined, closing about 1933.

Coal mining in and around Machen

There were several coal levels in the village: Pentwyn pit, the Bovil level in the Chatham area, Sun Vein level on the mountain west of Ffwrrwm farm, the new pit above the forge near Cwm Nofydd which was never worked (being eventually blown up), and Machen colliery, or old pit, by Green Row.

There was also a Vedw level near the Woodruff family home, originally called Birchwood House, adjacent to the railway which transported its waste on a dramroad via a bridge over the main road (the abutments of which still remain), through the old Tyn-y-waun field to an area behind the recreation ground known as 'The Strawberry Tip'.

Machen old pit

This was re-opened about 1900, and was still working in the early 1920s. The old pit (Machen colliery) had been worked on a small scale in the 1840s by the Rector of Machen, the Rev. Augustus Morgan, to supply coal for the lime quarry in Machen which was owned by his father, Sir Charles Morgan. It was the cause of dispute when the Tredegar Estate mineral agent completed a contract to lease it for fuller working in the 1850s, apparently against the wishes of the family. By 1860 the lessees were bankrupt and the venture ceased.

Machen old pit, adjacent to Green Row.

'When I was a little lad, William Spargo, who lived next door to us, was the engineer in charge [at Machen old pit]. He would take me sometimes to watch him working the machinery and bringing the cages up and down. I remember that the machinery was very spick and span, the brass work really looked like brass work. The outcrop ran quite a distance along Rhyd-y-Gwern lane, and there was an outlet pipe near Jane Ann's [Jane Anthony's] cottage.' [RH]

Jane Anthony's cottage prior to re-building. It is known today as 'Green Acres'.

'Steamy Green'

'One of the last men to work down there was Bill Green. His job was to supply enough steam to keep the underground fans operating. His mates would shout. 'More steam, Green' and in consequence he was known, and is still remembered as 'Steamy Green'.' [SG]

Treat a horse right

'My father, Sam Harris, was in charge of the horses that pulled the drams from the pit to the tip area above Glan-yr-Afon, long since levelled out for building. One horse, named Tiger, would not start work until it had been given a piece of chewing tobacco. On one occasion the overseer hit Tiger with a sprag which so aggravated my father that he punched the man telling him, 'No-one is going to treat my horse like that. I can get him to work without any of that'. He was instantly dismissed. His workmates came out in sympathy, and he was back in charge by the next day.' [WH]

The problem of water

'Father had his training as a fitter in the Machen locomotive works, and then worked at the pit attending to the pumps. They would call him out at all hours as there was always a problem there with water, which led to its closure.' [LR]

'Dad was down in the old pit when he was 14 years old, and he used to say he never worked out of water, he was always IN water. He was a strong boy, and once a week he went with the overman to check the air shaft which was quite a distance from the pit entrance. They walked up to their armpits in water, and when they reached the bottom of the shaft, he had to lift the overman in a bucket to check that it was free. The job done, they would retrace their steps, once again through water. He also told me that in 1916, when they decided to pay him a man's wage, he couldn't follow any of the discussion because it was all in Welsh.' [JW] My grandfather was a roller in the tin works. He didn't want my father to work there because the conditions were so horrendous, but father used to say he obviously had no knowledge of underground working or he wouldn't have sent him there. [[JW]

'It always amazes me when I think back that there were no accidents there because the shaft was only covered with slats of wood. You could see the water underneath. Later Ted Davies built his bungalow right over the shaft, having first concreted it.' [KC] The bungalow was appropriately named 'Minehead' but today, after extensive alterations, it is known as 'The Ranch'.

The Bovil level was at the top of Llanarth Street in Chatham, adjacent to the old Rumney tramroad. It was first worked by Zephaniah Williams, one of the Chartist leaders in the 1820/30s who lived in the nearby Bovil House. This level, together with the Sun Vein level, also referred to as the Bovil Sun level, does not appear to have been operating at all this century although it is recorded as working in 1893. The English Methodist chapel can be seen in front of the Crown Inn. Both no longer exist.

Walking thousands of miles to work

Pentwyn colliery was a drift mine which was working in the early 1920s employing twenty to thirty men. The owners were the Pentwyn Black Vein Colliery Co. When it closed about 1923, many Machen colliers had already gone to Bedwas colliery which raised its first coal in 1912, while others walked over the mountain to the colliery at Nine Mile Point. Some walked thousands of miles in all weathers during their working lives to reach their workplace. One of these was 'Snooky' Jones who was reckoned to have covered 51,000 miles in crossing the mountain to work and back.

'There were always disputes at Nine Mile Point. There were ten children in our family, six boys and four girls. I can remember we would stand outside the back door, and if the hooter went once, it meant there was work, and if it went twice there was no work. I have seen my mother in tears many times when it was blew twice. I wanted to try for the scholarship at Maesycymmer, but my father said I had to stay at home and help her.' [DV]

Machen Quarry early this century. The last of the 'old' industries remaining in Machen today. In the 1800s it was part of the Tredegar Estate with kilns above Quarry corner.

Lime kilns and quarry

Archdeacon William Coxe travelling through Machen in 1801 commented: 'We passed through Machen Hill, whose steep side is almost covered with lime kilns appearing like small caves in the rock… it contains small amounts of zinc and lead, but is rich in the best coal which is in much demand for the furnaces and brass manufactures. It abounds also with limestone, which forms a considerable branch of traffic in these parts for the purpose of manure (burnt lime).' [WC]

The National Monuments Record inspector writes in 1967: 'There are four or five pairs of kilns situated on the hillside above Castell Meredyth (sic) adjacent to the quarry. There are traces of tracks or cartways at the back of them. This must have been an important site because I have never seen so many grouped together before.'

By the 1880s Mr Little of the Bovil farm was leasing the quarry from the Tredegar Estate and raising stone for road building with the aid of a mechanical crusher. In 1882-83, some 33,000 tons of crushed stone went by rail to the Maerdy area of the Rhondda. At that time between 60 and 70 men were employed. Messrs Watkins and Christopher trading as The Machen Stone and Lime Company were established in 1920, and in 1933 the name was changed to Machen Quarries Ltd, who modernised the machinery and greatly increased production. By 1950 this had risen to 50,000 tons of crushed and coated material being produced annually. At this time the company was still in private ownership.

Machen is now the only rail-linked quarry operating in South Wales.

Machen quarry, c. 1940. From left to right, back: Arthur Matthews (The Oak), Terence Davies, Dai Jones, Tommy Young. Front: Vic Matthews, Arthur Matthews (Channel View).

Modernisation of Machen quarry

In 1957 Lord Brecon acquired a controlling interest, and plans were made to install a completely new plant. This was to make the quarry a forerunner in automated quarry plant. Later mergers with Vaynor Quarries of Merthyr Tydfil and Powell Duffryn led to Machen Quarry trading as Vaynor Quarries Ltd. During the 1970s and 1980s Powell Duffryn (Quarries) Ltd was formed, to be followed by ARC Powell Duffryn Ltd, the latter being one of the largest quarrying groups in the United Kingdom. The old Machen quarry today is known as ARC South Wales Ltd, Machen Quarry. It now covers approximately 150 acres of hard magnesium limestone which is won from a rising hillside, the strata of which inclines at an angle of 40 degrees falling from south to north. It is developed into 'benches' which range from 5' to 60' in height. The present crusher reduces stone to market requirements, one third of which is produced for British Rail for ballast. Stone from the quarry is supplied from 10-ton blocks for sea defences down to fine dust, the whole of the crushing and screening plants being operated from a central control room. In addition, a new plant has been erected at a cost of over £2 million which produces coated roadstone at a rate of 150 tonnes per hour. There is a work force of 44, a high percentage of whom live in the locally.

'On returning to spend my 91st birthday in Machen in 1993, I was able to compare the scene at the quarry today with my boyhood memories. We drove to the top and stopped to look at the workings below and the immense crushing plant. I remembered the simple crushers, driven by a steam engine, served by a narrow tramway which was all the equipment there when I was a boy.' [AJ]

'We always called it 'the lime kills' where we were sent to fetch lime. You bought so many pounds of lime, poured on the boiling water and it used to bubble up and then we used to white lime everywhere.' [LR]

Waterloo Works

Workers at Waterloo Tinplate Works, 1920s. The men from left to right are: Bernal Rodway, Shadrach Banfield, Bob Banfield, Bert Rodway. The women are Annie Jones and Olive Bond. Note the hand leathers which women needed for protection when splitting sheets. The 'Waterloo' commenced working in 1876 and at one time was part of Machen Iron and Tinplate Works (the old forge). When the latter closed down in 1887 the Waterloo continued until closure in 1941 producing tin-plate for metal containers of all types, although on one occasion, a former employee Mr Doug Hufton remembers a contract for India which was to build complete houses of metal. Although in Rudry parish, this concern employed many Machen workers. People employed from the surrounding area numbered about 250, and the processes required protective clothing to combat the terrific heat generated from the hot metal. A special boot or clog with a steel sole was worn by the doubler and his first helper for folding the hot sheets during rolling. Mill workers had to fold brown paper or newspaper round their boots, kept in place by string to protect their feet, white duck aprons were worn to protect legs and towels around the neck were used to wipe away sweat.

The owners for many years prior to closure were Partridge Jones and John Paton Ltd. The works weathered periods of recession in the 1930s, but the opening of the Ebbw Vale Strip Mill followed by the Rogerstone Aluminium Works in 1938, both of which could produce a better product with vastly improved machinery, proved too much, coupled with the outbreak of war, which made exporting very difficult. Like the old Machen forge there is now little to show that this tinworks ever existed.

Cray Valley Products

The Cray Valley factory at the Waterloo site opened for business in 1952. It became known locally as the 'Paint Works' although paint was never manufactured there. The resins which it manufactures have a wide variety of applications, including printing inks, paints, varnishes, adhesives etc. It was the brainchild of John Coates, head of Coates Brothers, which had started with John & George Coates manufacturing printing inks in 1877 at a site in Clapham, London. The 52-acre site borders the River Rhymney, which was diverted to permit building with the ground being raised by eight feet to minimise the risk of flooding. Even so, in 1962, the river broke its banks and flooded the site, causing widespread damage. The factory's products are used in food packaging, printing on beverage cans, newspapers and magazines, as well as normal domestic decorative paints and wood varnishes. The resins for protective coatings developed by Cray Valley can be found on objects as diverse as Concorde and the Eiffel Tower. They travel from Machen to Newport, or even Tokyo – in fact, to all four corners of the world. The most notable innovation, amongst many developed at Machen, has been thixotropic resins, which are used in non-drip paints.

In 1990 Cray Valley became part of the worldwide Total Group of companies, and Machen was chosen as the location for the Headquarters and Technology Centre of the Coatings Resins Department. Cray Valley currently employs in excess of 250 people at Machen, many of whom live locally. Also manufacturing on the Waterloo site, through historical links with the Coates Group, are the Valspar Corporation who have approximately 50 employees at Machen involved in the production of coatings for the metal packaging industry. In the third picture note the slag heap containing waste from Bedwas Pit.

Two
Tramroads and Railways

Machen has had railways in one form or another for more than 300 years. Railed waggon ways had been in existence from the end of the seventeeth century and consisted of two sets of wooden rails, each with a groove for the wheels. Later the rails were made of iron bolted to large stones which were used as sleepers. Other methods, known as inclined planes, required no expensive power to operate them. Often inclined planes were used as feeders to a main line. Two parallel sets of rails were laid down a slope and, with trams or drams connected by ropes, a full dram going down the slope would pull an empty, lighter dram, up to the top. There was one such incline over the other side of the mountain to the canal near Risca at Waun Fawr when Machen parish extended to the River Sirhowy. Another incline operated by gravity from Pentwyn pit above Cwm Nofydd to the railway at the forge. Here, however, a stationary engine at the pit pulled the empties back up.

The Coming of the Railway

The Old Rumney, as it was called, still had horse-drawn coal trams but, with gigs, carts and pedestrians also using it as a highway, because of the bad condition of roads, it became very congested. This line followed the eastern side of the Rhymney valley from the ironworks at Rhymney, through Bedwas and Machen to join the Monmouthshire Tramway at Tydu (Bassaleg). It became the Rumney Railway Company in 1861 with the intent of adapting to passenger traffic. However, the Brecon and Merthyr Railway Company, incorporated in 1859, bought the Rumney and made modernisation a priority. An Act of Parliament in 1864 approved deviations at Bedwas and Machen, and the work involved relaying most of the line to replace the mix of edge rails and flanged rails. This applied particularly to a major diversion at the Rising Sun (Graig-y-Rhacca Curve) which has now largely disappeared under the present Graig-y-Rhacca housing estate. While this work was in progress, lack of money and the continuing use of the line for coal traffic, prevented the early introduction of passenger traffic. This eventually came about in June 1865.

'A plain representation of the teams and trams of coal brought down to Pillgwelly by Samuel Homfray Esq., on Tuesday 8th December 1821'. This oil painting (c. 1821) by I. Thomas was originally housed in Lower Machen School House. It is reproduced here by permission of the Welsh Industrial and Maritime Museum.

The entrance to the culvert at White Hart.

David Jones and the Brecon & Merthyr

The civil engineer employed by the Brecon & Merthyr (B. & M.) to carry out the work of upgrading the railway was David Jones, whose son inherited his engineering expertise, becoming deputy superintendent of the B. & M. Railway, and manager of the Machen locomotive shops where many engineers were trained. David Jones was meticulous in recording the events relating to this project, and copies of his letters in Newport Reference Library, although faded, are mostly legible. One problem concerned access at White Hart and in one of his letters to the company, Jones wrote:

'As this matter may come to some expensive litigation... it is worth making a culvert 26 feet long 4 feet wide and 5 feet 6 inches high under the line in front of the Forge Hammer. The place is most favourable to make such opening. I feel it is my duty to lay before you what the

dependent Iron Master & Coal Merchant, ... neighbourhood of Newport by reducing the Price ... humble Servant Iu: Thomas. Samuel Homfray Esq. on Tuesday 18 Dec. 1821 Weight of Coal, 79 Tons 10 Cwt

probable expense will be if this little job is not done. Two public houses and about a dozen workmen's cottages will have claims against the company.'

David Jones planned and constructed the line of 3.75 miles that ran from Machen to Caerphilly, which became part of the Brecon & Merthyr railway, at a cost of £11,199. 9s 0d. The branch, as it was known, was fine for traffic heading towards Caerphilly, but the gradient into Machen of 1:39 was too great to permit heavy loads travelling from Caerphilly so a loop line, with a ruling gradient of 1:200, was built from Gwernydomen to Machen; this opened in 1891. David Jones records that 500 Irish labourers and masons were employed in the construction of the loop with labourers getting 3/- per day, and masons 6/-per day. There is a field near Pentwyn pit, where these employees lived, which to this day is called 'The Irish Field' where a clay pipe has recently been found bearing the symbol of an Irish harp and a Gaelic inscription.

Viaduct on the branch line, adjacent to Machen Forge and Tin Works.

Gwernydomen halt, situated on the junction between branch and loop line, was built in 1904 together with halts at Waterloo and Fountain Bridge. Photograph by Ian Wright.

The 'Motor' at White Hart halt which was opened in 1947.

There were two B. &. M. Stations in our area; one in Machen and the other, Church Road Station, in Lower Machen. Both of them were opened for passengers between Newport and Brecon in 1865. Before the arrival of omnibuses, the railway was a vital service for local people, who would travel to do their shopping and visit the markets at Newport, Caerphilly and Pontypridd.

Machen station was a basic building with ticket office, waiting-room and goods shed, with a shelter on the down side. As it was now a junction it had several sidings. The station siding was used by coal merchants – the local coalmen – with horses and carts. One of these was Stan Thomas. Photograph from the R.W. Kidner Collection (1910).

Stan Thomas's coal lorry in The Crescent.

'My father [Stan Thomas] went to work as a miner in Machen old pit at the age of twelve, and from there to pits higher up the Rhymney Valley. During the strikes of the '20s he left the pit and started his own business as a coal merchant and haulage contractor with a horse and cart. In those early years, he employed on a part-time basis many of the Minty boys: Trevor, Ralph, George and Arthur. Later George became a permanent worker. Dad later bought a lorry, and George became the driver.' [MW]

The colliers' train was always parked in the north siding. It was just a stark wooden train, no padding inside, and when it was left overnight, we kids would go and play. There was no vandalism, it was just a great place to play and no-one bothered about us.' [MH]. Photograph by Michael Hale. On the right is the top line to Brecon, the middle line is the loop line from Caerphilly and, to the left, is the branch line from Machen to Caerphilly. In the foreground are the rails leading to the coal-merchants' siding.

Church Road station. The station building was a fine example of the B. & M. architecture, and had a siding into a goods yard equipped with a crane. There was also a cattle pen. Photograph by Lens of Sutton.

'Church Road station' started life as a small halt used a great deal by those living at Ruperra Castle. Members of the Morgan family, visitors, servants who were employed from far away, and goods for Ruperra, all used to get off at Church Road.' [DB]

'My mother, Margaret Thomas, was the district nurse and midwife. She brought many Machen babies into the world. One night she had delivered one of the Price children, and prepared to walk home late to Upper Machen. Charlie Price said to her, 'Don't let anyone know I've done this', putting her up in the engine cab, and arranging for a driver to take her home.' [MR]

The Sheds (shops)

The B. & M. carriage works in Machen developed from a repair yard of the old Rumney originally built by them in 1870 and extended in 1900, 1911 and 1922. It covered a large area of 23,523 sq. ft. when merged with the Great Western Railway in 1922. Apart from building, repairing and maintaining engines, it produced first-class engineers who were sought after in many fields of engineering after their apprenticeships at Machen. The apprenticeship system trained coppersmiths, boiler makers, blacksmiths, coach painters, fitters and turners, many of whom became marine engineers serving in ships all over the world.

The remains of the repair shops in 1949 (photograph by Oakwood Press). After closure many workers transferred to the GWR workshops in Caerphilly and Swindon. Two carriages of men would travel from Machen to the Caerphilly sheds on the train leaving at 6.55 a.m. and returning at 5.15 p.m. daily. Many others moved to the West Midlands, finding lucrative work in the car industry. The sheds closed about 1927 but were used during the war for storage of timber from Cardiff to lessen fire risk from air raids. The gantry was not removed until after the war.

Bovil House. This was built by Llewelyn Llewelyn, a Mynyddislwyn farmer, for his daughter who was married to Zephaniah Williams, one of the Chartist leaders. By the 1860s it had become the official residence of a number of the B. &. M. superintendents: John Brewer, the agent for the old Rumney tramroad; G.W. Owen, who was run over by a train near to the house; and James Dunbar, until his death in 1922.

Mr Rogers' team of mules which were housed at White Hart.

A mule's sense of time

'Old Mr Rogers had a team of mules. They would be cutting down the trees for pit props [during the First World War]. You'd see them coming down through the Ruperra wood with bundles on each side of their bodies, eight or nine of them, all one after the other tied together, like. They'd walk all the way to Church Road station [the props would go on to Newport], then they'd come back to Machen. These old mules knew when their finishing time was coming and when they got to The Tredegar Arms they stopped for old Mr Rogers to go in, and would go off up to the White Hart, under the arches, and go home on their own. I know that for a fact – I'd be in school and you'd see the mules outside.' [LR]

A train out of the Wild West

'It was a busy line in 1918, train after train loaded with coal descending slowly to Newport Docks, interspersed with passenger trains. One about 12.30 was taken by us [working at Nantygleisiad] as our dinner bell, as we carried no watches. About every two hours a train, owned by the Alexandra Docks and Railway Company, passed on its way between Machen and Pontypridd via Caerphilly. This train consisted of a small engine and two coaches only, but they were strange ones. They were long and had straw-pleated seating ranged down the sides with a wide central passage, and at the ends they had open observation platforms on which I loved to ride. Some years later I recognised them in Wild West films, and later still, I learned that they had been brought to this country by Barnum and Bailey's circus and left behind when the circus returned to the USA.' [AJ]

Coal train on the loop line at White Hart. Photograph by Michael Hale.

First-class travel

'When I was a little girl I always wanted to ride in a first-class carriage on the train. One day my chance came. Mother took me with her to Newport to pay the account for the iron [father was the blacksmith] and he gave me a whole half-a-crown for myself. I walked to Machen station and bought a first-class ticket for the mile trip to Church Road, was taken by the station-master to the carriage, the door closed, and on that journey I tried each one of the upholstered seats in turn. When the train arrived at Church Road, Mr Price came up to the carriage, and opened the door for me. I think they phoned him from Machen station to tell him I was coming. The family thought I was mad. It cost me 6d and I've never forgotten it.' [MJ, c. 1914]

Pigeons

'One thing I always remember was the pigeons. There were always baskets of pigeons on the platform at Machen station waiting to be transported to faraway places for different races.' [AR]

Trethomas and Machen gangs relaying the track on the Fountain Bridge in the 1920s. Among those pictured are George Prince, Alfie Morgan, Ivor Horton, Dil Davey, Eli Coleman, Inspector Stephen, John Coleman and Charlie Harris.

Working for the GWR

The railway employed a great many people. There were the station-master, signalman, booking clerk, porter and teams of workmen who were maintaining the track. The ganger in charge of such a group would walk up to sixteen miles a day to inspect the keys and chairs. It was not a highly paid occupation, but it did have the advantage of a small pension, free passes and privilege tickets which entitled families to cheap transport dependent on the number of years the breadwinner had been employed. An extra pass could be earned if he completed first-aid courses for which special certificates and badges were given. A free pass (three a year) allowed the employee, plus wife and children, to travel anywhere on the GWR at no cost. The first-aid pass allowed free travel on all main domestic railways (at that time LNER, LMS, Southern including Southern Railway-owned boats to the Channel Islands). Privilege tickets gave travel at half-price; for example, an adult privilege fare to Cardiff via Caerphilly pre-war was 8d and a child's: return 4d.

Life at Church Road Station.

By 1891 Church Road was a recognised station, complete with waiting-room and a telephone kiosk. The station-master then was Thomas Price, whose son Charlie Price followed him, remaining there until the early 1930s.

'Father [Charlie Price] was born in the station-house, and so were all of us children. He was very strict, everything had to be polished, and sometimes he would send the porter, Billy Lloyd, home because he hadn't cleaned his shoes. Lord Tredegar would get on the train at Bassaleg and get off at Church Road, and father would meet him and take him to the waiting-room for him to "doll up" in his hunting clothes. The carriage from Ruperra would be waiting outside with the coachman and valet. There were travelling rugs on the seats, and white sheets over them so that no fluff from the rugs got on to his red jacket or white breeches. He knew every one of the hounds by name. Father was a wonderful gardener, and he had 108 rose bushes all along the platform. On the down platform was a model of the church in flowers. When we used to come home on the train, people would ask us if we lived there, and could they have a bunch of flowers. On Good Friday, when there were no trains, he would start making the outline. It was on a slope and made of slate. He would build it up with 'snow-on-the-mountain' coming all over the top. Then he would get lots of stones and put them in buckets of water with bleach until they were white and use them to edge round it.' [DB]

'Mother and me went to Church Road to see Barnum and Bailey at Newport, but could not get in the train, had to drive into Newport, train crowded ... Joseph Spooner brought ferrets from Church Road station for Colonel Morgan, and Mr Rymer trucked 945 bushels of wheat to Church Road... Hauled basic slag today from Church Road.' [Extracts from the diary of WB, kept from 1899 to 1919]

The Pontypridd to Machen passenger service ceased in 1956. Church Road station closed in September 1959, to be followed by Machen station on 31 December 1962. The latter continued for goods until July 1964, and remained a while after that for bulk freight.

Machen station

Our station has closed, the rails shine no more,
The platforms are empty, and crumbling away,
But I still give thanks for my memory's store.

'In '14 your Dad went from there to war'
Mam said, 'and we sat in Chapel to pray',
Our station has gone, the rails shine no more.

Then did I learn what it was to be poor,
Strikes and depression, no work and no pay,
But I still give thanks for my memory's store.

'Up on the truck, Jack, throw down the black ore,
Bag up enough to last yet one more day',
Our station has gone, the rails shine no more.

Better times now, trips to town and sea shore,
Dad's passes allowed us to play, laugh and stay,
But I still give thanks for my memory's store.

Nigh on a century it served us before
It fell to a land of waste and decay.
Our station has gone, the rails shine no more,
But I still give thanks for my memory's store.

[DC]

Three
Agriculture

Archdeacon William Coxe said of Machen when he passed through in 1801 that it was 'sprinkled with neat farm houses, in the midst of inclosures of corn and pasture. This district is extremely fertile and well-cultivated and yields more corn, in proportion to its extent, than any other part of Monmouthshire'.

The Morgans of Tredegar owned most of Machen, which was only one part of their vast holdings in Monmouthshire, Glamorganshire and Brecknockshire. The ancient farms of Cwm Nofydd, Gelliwastad and Rhyd-y-gwern are mentioned in the Tredegar Estate archives in the National Library of Wales at Aberystwyth as far back as the late 1400s, the name Pennelanne (Pen-y-lan) can be found in 1510, while Machen Plas was built by Thomas Morgan shortly after the battle of Bosworth Field in 1485, at which he fought for Henry Tudor (Henry VII) and was well-rewarded for his loyalty.

Machen Plas built by Thomas Morgan, Esquire of the Body to Henry Tudor. His branch of the Morgan family was resident for four generations moving to Tredegar House *c.* 1655.

Machen House built on the site of the original Machen Rectory in 1831 for Augustus Morgan, Rector of Machen, third son of Sir Charles Morgan of Tredegar House.

The Tredegar Estate

The Tredegar Estate, which had influenced the lives and fortunes of so many in Machen, began to decline after the First World War. The need to pay very severe death duties, coupled with the fact that rents over the previous century had never been realistic in view of rising taxation, brought about the need to realise capital. The income from the industrial assets was subsidising the agricultural side of the estate and 1925 saw the sale of many properties in the village to be followed by more in 1938, 1940 and 1943. The final sale, so far as it concerned Machen, was in 1956 to the Eagle Star Insurance Company who in most cases offered tenants the chance to purchase. From 1918 to 1938 the agent for the Estate was Mr Leonard Foster Stedman who was knighted in 1937. He lived at Machen House for nine years until his retirement in 1938 and identified a great deal with village life. The works office and yard was in Rhiwderin, from where the estate craftsman would be sent to deal with any repairs required on the farms. The yard was established on the site of the disused Rhiwderin Tin Works in 1899, and plasterers, carpenters, plumbers, masons, glaziers, roofers, painters and gate-hangers were all based there, together with apprentices and labourers. One of their most important tasks was the hanging and maintaining of gates, since Lord Tredegar was a keen huntsman, and he expected to be able to follow his hounds without having to get off his horse. Latches had to be lifted with the stock of his whip.

The Tredegar Hunt meeting at The Ffwrrwm Ishta, 1957.

'My great-grandmother used to repair the red hunting coats for Lord Tredegar which my great-grandfather Whittingham had made. He was a tailor at Twynsych [now in ruins] where he did his sewing sitting cross-legged on the table. The coats were brought for repair by a footman on horseback, but when repaired my grandmother and great-grandmother would walk via Rhyd-y-gwern lane to Ruperra Castle to return them. They were paid and given tea in the castle kitchens and then had to walk all the way home.' [MW]

'Amongst the many highlights of childhood memory, were visits, made in the afternoon of St David's Day, to the summer-house on the ancient hill-fort above Ruperra Castle. I can still smell, as I write, the sickly-sweet perfume of the rhododendrons as we crossed the iron bridge by the Michaelstone road, and the bunches of snowdrops we picked on the way back home'. [EJC]

'When gates were put in on the farms, two men would come from the estate yard, and they would take all day to do the job, and when it was complete the letter 'T' was incised on them. My grandmother would make Caerphilly cheese, and the miners would call to buy the wet cheese to take with them down the mine. What she did not sell to them she would take to the market at Caerphilly. She also churned butter and as there was no greaseproof paper in those days, she would take a sycamore leaf from one of the many trees round the farm, and lay the pat of butter on that, it looked very nice and kept cool. In the old days a lot of the work was done by casual labour, not many farms had permanent workers. There was a lot of poverty, and my father used to say when he did his milk round he saw many children who had no shoes.' [JT]

'One of the great achievements in recent years has been the eradication of TB [tuberculosis] in dairy herds, 50 to 75 per cent of which were infected. No wonder that TB was rife in the 1930s and 1940s.

The most important improvement on this farm [Cwm Nofydd] was the coming of water and electricity. We were often short of water, and had to go to a well in the wood for drinking water in the house, while the animals had to be taken down to the river. Electricity came here in 1947.' [JT]

The Tredegar Estate sale of 1956 not only made it possible for many tenants of farms and cottages to buy their freeholds, but it paved the way for the extensive forestry which is now part of the mountain landscape. The Forestry Commission followed the Eagle Star Insurance Company in offering to buy the rough land at between £5 and £10 an acre which helped the tenants in their purchase and the Commission to proceed with afforestation. The area on Mynydd Machen behind the Vedw and in front of the old coal tips has been planted with Japanese Larch, Lodgepole Pine, Scots Pine and Norway Spruce, and now presents an attractive backcloth of forest and grassland.

Sizeable areas of farmland have been used for building and many of the small farms have now become residential dwellings with their acreages being attached to larger farms. This applies to Nantygleisiad, Blaen-y-cwm, Ty Draw, Ty Pwca, Mary Ann Jones's land, Penllwyn, Graig-y-Rhacca, Pentwyn, Ysgubor Fach, Ysgubor Fawr and Rhyd-y-gwern. Bovil farm, Bovil Uchaf and Ffwrrwm farm are now in ruins, and their land is used for sheep farming.

Ffwrrwm farm 1977. The land is now attached to Park farm.

Bovil farm 1977. It is now farmed with Tyn-y-Ffynnon.

Farming enters the machine age

Farming methods were to change drastically after the outbreak of war in 1939. Up to that time ploughing was done with horses. If it was a single plough, two horses would be used, but if it was a double plough there would be three horses walking abreast, or sometimes one in front, and two behind. Scythes were used for harvesting. They were set by the blacksmith to the size of the men using them. Hedge-laying was done by hand, but with the grubbing out of hedges to create larger, more 'efficient' fields, this is an art that is on the wane. Mowing machines with finger-like blades which moved sideways took over from scythes, and from about 1970 machines worked with a rotary action having large discs.

With the need to grow as much as possible in wartime, more land was put down to arable, and farm machinery became more commonplace. Farmers were more or less forced to buy tractors in order to get the percentage of ground ploughed as demanded by the War Agricultural Department. The first tractors in Machen were a small Allis Chalmers bought by Elias John at Machen Plas and a Fordson Major bought by Henry John at Park farm, both in 1940. Cwm Nofydd had a Massey Harris. On farms with dairy herds, hand-milking was still the pattern during the war. The Alfa Laval milking machines were introduced in 1942 and since some farms did not have electricity until the 1950s these were powered by petrol engines.

'The most useful improvement on our farm has been the tractor. We went from horse and cart to the tractor, and the early ones were open to the weather, and had cleats on the wheels. If you wanted to go out on the road you had bands to fit and bolt on. Nowadays, they are weatherproof, computerised, very comfortable, and different attachments can be added.' [RJ]

Jack John's butcher's trap from Pen-y-Parc (Park farm), *c.* 1920. The John family settled there in 1893. Many descendants still live locally.

Milk production

'They had a pedigree dairy herd at Machen House when I was young, and every Sunday you could go down there and buy skimmed milk. We would take a bottle, and it was one penny a pint.' [KP]

'The change in dairy farming came when 'the small man' was pushed out about the late '60s because the churn collection from the wooden stands at the side of the road ceased, and they went over to bulk tanker collection. My uncle had a milk round in Machen up to 1920. Then my father took it over until about 1933. He would also carry eggs and Caerphilly cheese that my mother made. We took milk to Cardiff in churns to the Meadowland dairies, twice a day because there was no refrigeration and they wanted fresh milk. They were the old-fashioned churns with big bottoms tapering to the top, and held 17 gallons. Later, we transferred to Jones in Rhiwderin, and were given petrol coupons during the war to cover running the tractor, milking machines etc., [Petrol rationing ceased in 1950]. Eggs went to the packing station at Llanishen in crates holding 30 dozen. [RJ]

Sheep sales

'Machen, like many other areas, used to have sheep sales about the middle of September. The flocks were walked, not transported, to the back of the Ffwrrwm, just a little paddock behind. All farmers sold their draft sheep, probably three to four-year-olds… most hill farmers sold their surplus sheep at the sales. I am going back to about 1930, possibly before that. I had a day off school and my job was to chase the sheep off the mountain, run in front and close all the gates.' [RJ]

Hay making at the Gelli, late 1920s.

'You musn't judge a 'oss by his 'arness'

'Morgan Bla'ncwm was a character. He farmed up on the mountain, and he let his sheep wander all over the village. People would go on at him about their vegetables and flowers being eaten, and he would say 'never mind, it won't hurt 'em'. [Another version was 'Never mind, girl, it be like cake to 'em, see, like cake'. Morgan Bla'ncwm would start off with about 40 sheep and end up at the sale with 20, the others would be in somebody's garden or the churchyard!] One day he was down in the village for one of the horse sales held at the Ffwrrwm. He was pretty untidy, his dress was terrible. He bought a horse, and the auctioneer said 'Will you sign? Can you write, old man?' He signed with a flourish. 'You certainly can write, old man' and Morgan answered, 'You mustn't judge a 'oss by his 'arness.' He could write the most beautiful copper-plate.' [IR]

Threshing time at Pen-y-lan, early 1900s.

Pandy mill, 1970. The Pandy mill and Machen corn mill were part of the agricultural scene. The Pandy and the corn mill, situated a little futher along the valley, used the same leat and there were frequent problems with flooding.

The Pandy mill

This is described in a lease of 1708 as three houses, one tucking mill, two barns, orcharding and seventeen acres of land. 'Pandy' is Welsh for a fulling or tucking mill which thickened and shrunk the cloth woven by the local weavers. After this was done the cloth was stretched out on tenter frames, the cloth being attached to the frame by 'tenter hooks' from whence the saying originates. The field adjacent to the Pandy is named 'Cae'r Ddayntir' on the Machen Tithe Map (1841). By the early 1800s the mill was making manufactured goods from its cloth, and William Jones, who also ran the Castle mill at Caerphilly, was noted as a weaver, and later as a woollen manufacturer at the Pandy, Machen, from about 1840 until his death in 1869. He was a bard with the name Gwilym Ilid and was regularly nominated in Machen vestry minutes to serve as parish constable. He was followed by David Lewis and his son Thomas as tenants.

The blacksmith at Lower Machen made various parts of machinery for the 'Pandy factory' including bands and tie-bolts for the floodgates. At other times tools were made for disconnecting the water-wheel, levers to raise the flood gates and bars to form a grating for the wheel. The latter item required 125 lbs of iron while the flannel tenters needed 51 feet of chain, six dozen bolts, and 150 feet of plating with nails and pins. The interior machinery also required maintenance; pulleys needed new straps, set pins were broken, rollers needed re-soldering and brackets were made for the power-looms. What a sight it would have been to see the whole process taking place!

The mill was wound up in 1903, although the machinery remained in situ for some years. The stock list at that time shows shirts at 5/6, drawers at 2/11, stockings at 1/6, together with wool of different types, dyes, oils and soaps. Items of machinery included a handmule, looms, boilers and kilns. Today the site is occupied by a modern residence, the old buildings that remain bearing silent testimony to an age when water power and skilled craftmanship were paramount.

The weir, early this century.

Fulling and weaving

'The hills of Machen were ideal for rearing sheep. There was a large amount of wool produced, and for years our fleeces from Nantygleisiad were sent down to the Pandy to be treated by Thomas Lewis. By 1891 he had retired and Daniel Jones from Llandysul [Cardiganshire] moved there. He was a complete fuller and weaver. My mother told me there were plenty of salmon in the Rhymney, and the Rev. Augustus Morgan used to take a salmon for the family breakfast from the weir near the mill and woe betide anyone caught poaching!' [MMJ]. DB's mother saw men catching salmon under the bridge by the old school.

Welsh 'flanning'

'Mother came this way when she was twelve from Cardy, Cardiganshire like, and they used to make the Welsh flanning [flannel] down there… and the big wheel was driven by water. There's a big weir there, a whirlpool, and in the middle of the river a lot of stakes. When they wanted more water, they used to barricade that off and turn it down the dykes with an oak board, deep and long, which they dropped in between the stakes and that went all the way to the Pandy. In the ground there were little cottages, my mother and others from North Wales, they used to live there. When it was going through the washing sort of thing, this wheel used to spin it round, not in one piece, it was a string all in lumps, and they was at the other end catching it, flattening it out, put through another machine and out came Welsh flanning.' [LJH]

'When I lived there, I remember walking down a long passage, looking through the gaps in the wooden ceiling to see the machinery. There were some sheds there and five great boilers, like the boilers we used to have for washing with the fires underneath, but much bigger. In Weavers' Row, where the Pandy weavers lived, people had to save their urine which was used to go on the flannel. [This was for the dyeing process to fix the colours. The urine pit remained for many years] [LR]

'My father told me he and other boys and girls used to bathe and paddle in the leat when he was about 10 [1903].' [EJC]

Daniel James and his wife who lived in Chatham Street dyed cloth which was made into shirts and together with knitted stockings, he would tie the garments on a stick which he carried over his shoulder trudging the valleys selling to housewives.

Machen corn mill, 1971. (Photograph, courtesy of Glyndwr G. Jones).

Machen corn mill

Little is known about this mill, although there is mention of a 'Maister's Mill' and 'Master's Mill' in leases from 1508 and in Land Tax records. Since most manors had their own corn mill, this could refer to an older mill. A map dated 1836 in the Tredegar archives shows that it belonged to Sir Charles Morgan together with the Pandy and had 25 acres of ground including Gwern-y-felin, the two fields which now comprise the recreation ground. The 1871 census mentions Henry Thomas in occupation and a Mrs Ann Davies in 1900, when it is referred to as Mill farm. It was used as a slaughter house by Mel Rees who had a butcher's shop in Machen, and has been owned for many years by the Llewellyn family.

'Grandfather told me that in his young days, the 1830s, the farmlands from Bedwas to Machen were covered with corn, but by 1936 only four acres of corn were growing in the same stretch of the valley. Milling ceased in the 1890s, the miller's son, Jack Davies, became a chief engineer at sea.' [MMJ]

Machen Show

An established part of the agricultural year is the Machen Show which commenced in 1941 and has gone from strength to strength ever since. At first they were primarily gymkhanas and horse shows held to raise funds for the Home Services Comforts Fund in aid of troops serving abroad but by 1950 the event had grown to embrace classes for foxhounds, pigs and sheep. In 1977 the show was moved to Mill farm a very much larger site. These days the space is fully taken up with trade stands and agricultural sections, a rural craft tent, horticultural and domestic classes in addition to the popular and traditional events.

Four
Shops and Trades

Machen today has four shops: the post office, Machen filling station (more affectionately known as the 'Old Post' which it once was), a unisex hairdresser's with boutique and a Chinese take-away. Those who were not born in the village or moved in from other areas in the 1950s and later, cannot imagine that in the early part of the century and up to the 1930s, there had been as many as fifty shops and three banks.

Up to the late 1920s most local shopping was confined to Machen with the 'town shopping' being done in Newport, Caerphilly and Pontypridd, all of which also had good markets. The availability of trains made this the main transport for most people. A local bus route between Machen and Caerphilly commenced in 1922, but it was some years later before a service was running to Newport. This began to affect local shops and businesses.

Russell House today. This is a double-fronted building in Commercial Road situated at the bottom of Alma Street. It was the original truck shop where workers at the tinworks were compelled to purchase their requirements by the use of tokens which were part of their pay. With more than 200 adults employed there, it was a most lucrative operation for the owner, Joseph Russell. It later developed into a small department store run by W.H. Davies, the prominent councillor and dignitary. It later became the residence and surgery of Dr C.E.P. Davies, and Dr J. Davies, son-in-law and grandson of W.H. Davies.

Commercial Road, *c.* 1900, showing Russell House with the projecting awning. Meyricks (opposite Siloam chapel) was a grocery shop that also stocked tobacco, corn, meal for poultry and items for heating and lighting. Originally started by James Meyrick early in the century, it was later run by his children. It had a bakehouse attached which was taken over in turn by Percy Cook and Emlyn Jones who baked and delivered bread from there until long after the shop had become a private dwelling. Percy's nickname was 'No Socks' since he never wore any, even in winter. He would catnap in his chair by the fire, seldom sleeping at night, since he was always baking for the next day.

Davies the Grocer

'One side was devoted to grocery, while the other side displayed bedding, curtains, dress materials and table linen. There was everything for a collier, tommy tins, jacks, boots hanging down from the ceiling, rows of materials, winceyette for children's nightdresses, shoes and beautiful dolls. Mr Davies had three daughters who served in the shop. They were all behind the counter dressed in white overalls. The old man was bald, and had a waxed pencil moustache. You never seen a mark on them girls, clean as a pin always.' [LAH, AR and LR]

Percy Cook's van behind Meyrick's shop.

Meyrick's shop

'Ernest and Alfred Meyrick and their spinster sister, Annie, ran it during the First World War. It was a very sociable shop, there was time for everybody. Annie provided the chatter, acted as finance officer, having custody of all receipts and making all change from a mouse-coloured, spongy money-bag which dangled about her ample midriff, supported by unbreakable thongs which were slung about her neck. Alfred used to bake "Turog bread" in a bakehouse shed at the back, and made regular deliveries about the village with a little horse and trap. He was also the village lamplighter, and would travel around on a rickety old bicycle every morning and evening supporting a short ladder, to carry out his duties.' [LS]

Ernest Meyrick had a fine voice and was a member of the Royal Welsh Male Choir which travelled to Chicago in 1893 to sing at the World Fair. Shortly afterwards the choir sang to Queen Victoria at Windsor Castle. Ernest had a photograph hanging in the dining room behind the shop to prove it!

'I worked there as a part-time assistant and errand boy at weekends earning 2/- plus two free suppers and one free dinner. Rice, flour, sugar, dried fruit, corn, peas etc., were all delivered to the shop in sacks and orders were weighed into bags. Bacon was cut into good thick slices with a sharp knife, butter was cut from a huge slab and patted into shape, while cheese was cleanly cut with wire. Biscuits were displayed in large square tins, some with glass lids, for the customer to make a choice, and they were weighed loose. In the granary adjoining the bakehouse, maize, wheat, oats, bran and barley meal were stored, and I had to weigh in small quantities for customers who kept chickens and pigs. We had no electricity or gas in our homes, so paraffin and candles were much in demand. [AJ]

Near Meyrick's was John Davies' butcher's shop shown here earlier this century. During the 1920s and '30s there were several more butchers in the village. Mr John and then Mel Rees had a shop on the corner of Forge Road, later taken over by Dave Willetts who moved the business from there to premises across the road next to Russell House. The last butcher in this shop was Mr Myers. Four doors away was another butcher's shop run by Billy Hicks. The last of this long line of butchers was Ken Llewellyn who was in business at 48, Commercial Road until 1992.

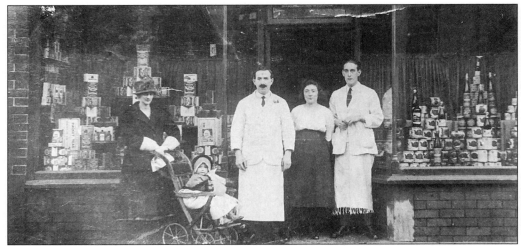

The Newport Industrial Co-operative Society shop ('The Kwop'). Situated on the main road opposite Lewis Street, this opened for business about 1905 continuing to trade until the mid-1960s. It stocked the range of a small department store, including millinery, clothes, and household linen. Today it has been converted into two flats.

'In the 1920s and '30s a bakery department was set up in the building at the back of the shop. Bread was delivered round the village then by horse-drawn van. The roundsmen I remember were Ted Brown, Ted James, Tom Prosser, and Arthur Richardson. They had two very important duties, firstly to take the horse to Lower Machen for shoeing by Bayliss (Bayley) Jones, this was usually every fortnight. Secondly, to deliver the groceries and bread to Mrs Burt at Bovil Uchaf every Thursday. The groceries were packed in two sacks, which were tied together and slung round the horse's neck. The horse was taken from the bread van at the Royal Oak, then led up the mountain where you were always given a warm welcome. In addition to this delivery, the errand boy carried four two-pound loaves up there every Monday. The dividend of one shilling in the pound was normally paid out quarterly, but quite a few left this to accumulate during the '20s and '30s to keep themselves afloat during the strikes of that period.' [HE]

An old view of Chatham. Woodruff's small shop in the main road served the Chatham area for several decades before closing about 1960. It was run by the wife of Lance Woodruff.

'I remember the poverty during the strike periods of 1926 and later, and I think there's a lot of kiddies in Chatham would have starved if it hadn't been for Mrs Woodruff and Mr Llewellyn [Mr Tom Llewellyn also kept a grocer's shop]. [RD]

'Mrs Woodruff was a plump lady who wore large wrap-around aprons which tended to wear in the middle. She would give these, when well-worn, to my mother and other women who had clever fingers to make them into dresses for their daughters.' [KP]

'Mrs Woodruff was there for years, through the strikes and depression, and into the days of rationing during and after the Second World War. We used to go and pay the bill every Friday night. We had it on tick all the week, and I would beam when Mrs Woodruff was serving. She would always give me a number of dolly mixtures for paying the bill. The only thing that got on my nerves with her was when she went to cut the bacon, she used to cross her knives back and forth to sharpen them, and it used to put my teeth on edge. As time went on she had a proper machine.' [VR]

The first recorded postmaster traced to date was William Grant in 1864. His daughter Mary was in charge up to 1888 when William Ebrill Edwards was appointed. After his death in 1933, his daughter-in-law carried on until 1949. The shop offered a vast range of services as, indeed, it still does today. It was a telegraph office, in addition to sorting and delivering mail, and supplied sweets, ironmongery items, grocery, small household goods, china and clocks which could be ordered, down to toys such as a child's rocking horse. The post office moved to 40 Commercial Road in January 1949 and was run by Mr and Mrs H. Thomas until 1971 when it moved to its present premises at Commercial Road under Mr A. Rogers. Its present-day postmistress is Mrs L. Greenhaf who was appointed in 1982.

'We never called the post office by its proper name, we simply said 'the post'. When I was asked to send a letter, I was told to hurry because the post goes at five o'clock. I stood opposite, outside the Ffwrrwm, and when the church clock struck five, the post didn't go – it's still there to this day!' [DH]

'When we took over the post office in 1949, we took over the responsibility for a 24 hour telephone service too. The telephone numbers ranged from Machen 01 (Cwmnofydd farm) to Machen 50 (Machen Quarry). As Machen Quarry had two lines, and there were two public telephones in the district, there were fewer than fifty subscribers in an area that extended as far as Ruperra Castle in one direction and The Rising Sun in the other. In those days it is amusing to recall that *The South Wales Argus* rang the police-station at Machen every evening. Very soon the policeman, who lived next door, would use us as an unofficial answering service when he had to go out. The call would come and in answer to the question 'Anything to report?', we would reply 'No, all quiet.' The conversation hardly ever varied. Every year at Christmas the Argus sent a chicken to each police-station in the county to thank them for acting as unoffical reporters throughout the year.' [DT]

'By 1971 the mail and counter services had been split up, and the mail sorting and delivery was transferred to a lock-up premises within the village hall. Also by this time telegrams had become a thing of the past. The major part of business concerned the paying out of pensions and other Social Security benefits, and the business connected with the GIRO Banking system.' [AR]

'In more recent times the person I remember most was 'Ralph the Post'. He always walked in the gutter, knew everyone by name, and could be relied on for a Woodbine or sweets. He wouldn't pass anyone by without offering them something.' [DW]

Lower Machen post office was located on the old road through Lower Machen, opposite the gates to the Old Rectory now known as Machen House. It later moved into one of the houses adjacent to the Forge, the home of the Beeston family for several generations.

'We always called it the pink shop. It was really a post office and general store. Tom Young had a slaughterhouse at the back. He cut his meat up on Friday and delivered it around locally by horse and trap on the Saturday with his dog, Rover, trotting behind. They sold everything, always the best quality and full of flavour. Later on, when the old post office closed, Mrs Beeston had it in her house nearby, and I did the round for years on my bicycle.' [MJ]

'The post was delivered by little, old-fashioned Lizzie Edwards and her sister Ginnie, two spinsters. They used to go round for years and years. Lizzie did it all her life. She walked miles and miles to the Home farm at Ruperra and all round the Draethen. She lived in one of the little mill houses.' [LR]

Dai Lewis' sweet shop in Lewis Street. There were many others who were content to make a simple living with their front-room shops, Mrs Sanders with her home-made cakes, Kate and Hilda Rees with their sales of newspapers, Wizard, Skipper and Hotspur comics and fireworks for bonfire night, were two examples.

A Sweet Life

'One shop was kept by a little old lady in the front room of her house. Her window displayed trays of sweets, none of them costing more than one penny for two ounces. We chose our sweets and she weighed them on her brightly polished brass scales, then taking a square of paper she fashioned it into a neat little cone-shaped bag, poured our sweets in and turned in the flap. Our pocket money was one or two pence a week, sometimes less, so we knew exactly what to buy. The halfpenny would buy one ounce of toffee, nougat, caramel, bonbons or liquorice ribbons. There were also the lucky bags, and one could become the possessor of a beautiful jewelled ring or bangle, or maybe a whistle. One penny would buy a whip and top.' [DD]

'I remember going with my friend, Cyrus Hughes, into Tom Llewellyn's shop and asking for a farthing's worth of sweets and please could we have them in two bags and WE GOT THEM.' [EJC]

Mr and Mrs E. Hartley at their sweet shop at 36 Commercial Road.

Forge Road today. The take-away was Berni's Café, the second shop was once a chemist. Its first tenant was Lewis John whose father built several houses along Commercial Road including the old police station and doctor's surgery,and the block at the top of Forge Road. He had a dairy there prior to 1920, and used to stable his horse at the back. It became a fish and chip shop, another chemist, and in recent years for a short while 'Anna the florist'. The third shop has been at different times a shoe repairer's, confectioner's, greengrocer's and lastly, a video rental shop. Berni's was a confectioner's shop and café run by the Berni brothers who were well-established by the 1920s. They also made delicious ice-cream which was taken around the village by hand-cart. One of their sons, Primo, grew up in Machen, and the family ran it for many years after the Second World War, but have now returned to Italy.

Berni's

'It was as much a social club as a shop. Before the war it was run by Vic Moruzzi, and it was a meeting place for all ages, where soft drinks, cordials, sarsaparilla and cream sodas could be purchased. I was a young married woman then with a baby son, and I used to go for many a walk along the lanes with Mrs Moruzzi who had just had her baby and could only speak Italian.' [KT]

'There was a pin table there, and you could sit for ages, even if you didn't buy anything, you were always welcome. They also sold chocolates as well as cigarettes and tobacco, but Berni's were of a particularly high quality. If you wanted something a little bit extra, it was the place to go to. I always remember that on Boxing Day morning up to mid-day, any man who went in and bought any tobacco, was always given a cigar.' [AR]

Clothiers

The village was well-catered for with regard to materials for dressmaking, and at 18 Commercial Road there was a gents' and children's tailoring shop run by a Mr Griffith. He was followed by Mr Doug John who later moved to Forge Road. There was a milliner, a Mrs Davies, in Lewis Street, and two shops selling wool, silks and haberdashery.

'Mr Doug John had an outfitter's shop opposite the church room. This was always well-stocked and he would buy in toys at Christmas time. All through the year starting in January, one could join the Christmas club with him. I remember going down there very well, just one or two pence a week, entered on the card and in his book. At Christmas time we would go and buy something, perhaps 1/6 might even buy a box of handkerchiefs for our fathers. We were sorry to see him close.' [AR]

'Doug John returned to Machen many years later. He called to see me and told me he wanted to see the old conker tree before he died. Both have now gone.' [KT]

Three in one

'Mrs Sarah Williams was a very astute shop-keeper. She had a haberdashery shop in Commercial Road selling wool, cottons, lace and embroidery silks. I loved going there, and used to save my pocket money for several weeks to buy silks. One day my grandfather had given me sixpence when he visited us, and I went to Mrs Williams for silks. She told me I was a good girl to save my money, and gave me an extra skein as a present. When my mother found I had an extra one, she took me back to make quite sure that there hadn't been a mistake. She always kept a jar full of ABC biscuits on the counter for children.' [KP]

'When children started going outside the village for secondary schooling, Mrs Williams branched out and stocked pens, pencils, inks, geometry sets, tracing paper and it was a service much used by local scholars. In addition, upstairs, her daughter Eleanor gave piano lessons, and from all accounts, she was an excellent teacher.' [AR] It is fitting that Eleanor's tombstone in St John's churchyard should have a treble clef as a motif to commemorate her musical talents.

'When I was little I remember a hatter and milliner's shop near Russell House run by one of the Potter family. There were high black silk hats for men, and the ladies' hats had big bunches of cherries on them. I did so wish I could have had some. In those days [early 1920s] important people always wore high top hats.' [LR]

Ironmongers

'There was an ironmongery and hardware shop in Commercial Road, next to Russell Stores, run by Jane Stephens, who later became the second wife of Mr G.D. Inkin, for many years headmaster of the school. It was a veritable gold mine, you could spend hours looking round there – it was something out of this world. Things hanging everywhere, there wasn't an inch to spare, pots, pans, old hanging lamps, bicycles. I had my first bike from there.' [AR]

Travelling greengrocery round from Lower Machen with George Baynton, 1930s. The village was well-supplied with visiting tradesmen.

Hawkers

'There was the shoni-onion man, wearing Breton blue jacket and trousers, always a beret, both riding and pushing his bike bedecked with ropes of onions on the handlebars. In those days, when Welsh was still spoken in the village, since the Breton language is so similar, there was more than formal conversation.' [EJC]

'I remember Mr Eaton coming up from Newport, selling paraffin off the back of his two deck Model T. Ford. He was a lovely fellow. He had a canopy over the top, and everything hanging all round it. He sold everything from a pin upwards and you paid him so much a week, no matter what you wanted. I've still got a tea set my mother bought off him, a dozen of everything.' [KP]

'When I was little, the cockle man would visit regularly from Newport in his trap piled with sacks of cockles. He would go into The Tredegar Arms, and his wife, poor woman, she'd be sitting up high on the seat in the trap, in the cold, waiting for the old man to come out.' [LR]

'Mr Gunn was a travelling man, who would visit the village before and after the war carrying goods wrapped up in two enormous carpet bags. He ran a club which enabled people to order clothes for which coupons were necessary for several more years before they were abolished for good. He was often referred to as 'the pack man.' Later on he had a car.' [KP]

Chemists

Years ago it was common practice for medicine to be dispensed by the doctor who would make up medicines and ointments in his surgery. There was a chemist on the main road opposite the conker tree rejoicing in the name of D.B. Screech, from which well-known proprietary brands could be obtained, for example: California Syrup of Figs, Parish's Food, Farley's Rusks, Scott's Emulsion and Malt together with castor oil, senna pods, iodine and sulphur and treacle which were regularly used for most ailments.

Fish and Chips

'There was always at least one fish and chip shop. I can name many of the people running them, Gimblett's, Martin's, Harris', Morris', Hartley's among them. The fish and chip shop run by Mr Gimblett in the 1920s was a very popular place since there were benches in the outside yard where we could sit and eat. A much visited fish and chip shop in later years was that of Ray Cook, a local man, situated at Trethomas which was very handy for those of us returning from the pictures at Bedwas Hall. Fish and chips there were one penny for chips and two pence the fish.' [AR and EJC]

Undertakers

The two men remembered by older residents in this connection were Tom Davies and Ted Phillips, both Machen born. They were skilled master carpenters, who were also cabinet makers and took orders for furniture, some of which has been handed down by their original owners to their children, such was the quality of the workmanship.

'Tom Davies, 'Tom the Funeral' as he was better known, had in his workshop tools hung at chest height above the long bench. There were eight or nine kinds of saws, from one-handed crosscuts to tenons, five or six kinds of hand planes, from a small steel type whose shaving surface could be curved, to a wood-block plane that was two feet long. The clay floor of the shop was always strewn with shavings. One day I told him I wanted to be a carpenter like Jesus. He exploded. 'It's only the pictures in Sunday school books that show him in the shop. Did he ever make anything? If I remember right, the only piece of wood Jesus talked about was a fig tree, and because it didn't have figs on it, he cursed it to death. Would a carpenter curse fig wood?' He would rent a hearse from Caerphilly, and with Bess the mare between the shafts, he would sit up with the driver, looking very distinguished in his tall silk hat.' [LS]

'My grandfather, Tom Phillips, was a carpenter and undertaker. He lived in Wyndham Street, and the old shed where he made the coffins is still there. We used to make the pillows with the wood shavings, and he had rolls of pretty material stacked up on the shelves which were sewn into shrouds. In the old days the coffin was usually left in the home before the funeral. I still have the special brass candle stick that he used to put on the coffin, and I remember that someone was always employed to sweep the road before the procession started.' [DB]

Shoemakers and Cobblers

These were very hard-working and skilled tradesmen, always in great demand. The names of Messrs Askey, Davies, Deacon, Hiscox and Purnell are still remembered today. They mainly repaired shoes, but most could, and did, make them. They had a wonderful facility in managing to keep a mouth full of sprigs which they spat out with great precision on to the leather.

'My grandfather explained that they put the nails in their mouth so that they would be wet, and when they went into the boot, they would rust and not fall out.' [LD]

'I remember the huge sheets of leather on the floor. On the bench were three lasts, large, medium and small, and behind was the sewing machine. This was well-used because hopscotch was a ruinous game on our toe caps. I loved to see him remove the worn toecap, replace it with a piece of soft leather, turn to his machine and stitch it into place, There were boxes of nails with the biggest box containing hobnails for the miner's pit boots. These were also just the nails for repairing spinning-tops which must have been a fiddling job, always done with good humour and no charge.' [DD]

Lower Machen forge. Bayliss (Bayley) Jones at work, with sons, Howard and Lloyd, and George Baynton. His father, Thomas, had been blacksmith and farrier here before him. There was also a wheelwright's shop attached. He started smithing in Upper Machen near the station before moving to Lower Machen in the 1890s, and died at the early age of 47 in 1910. His son, Arthur Bayliss Jones, carried on after him until the 1950s, assisted by his sons.

Lower Machen Forge

The forge was a busy place in the early part of the century, apart from shoeing the horses from the farms, and the mules used to transport wood, there were repairs to gates and farm tools, and a variety of items needed to keep the Tredegar Estate properties in good repair. Re-tyreing of wheels, making of firegrates, window hinges, hasps and bars, keys, scaffolding, and little jobs to help the housewife such as repairing kettles, shovels, and fitting handles to saucepans, not to mention making hoops and guiders for children were all part of the work at the smithy.

Tailoring and dressmaking – the Monkey House.

'This was the irreverent name given to the tailoring and dressmaking establishment in Commercial Road where I learnt my trade. It was run by Mrs Tom Jones in the '20s and '30s. She was an excellent tailoress and very strict with us. I went there for two years when I was fifteen. There were usually six of us, and we would sit on trestle-tables placed round the room with our work beside us. Mrs Jones had her table and chair in the centre close to the stove, and she always had a dish of nuts beside her which she dipped in salt. She started her business originally in Green Row. It gave us the chance to opt out of domestic service which was usually the only other work in those times. I went on to work at David Morgan's department store in Cardiff and it was due to her good grounding in sewing that I got a job there. They say it was called 'the monkey house' because people waved to us when they passed by.' [ID]

Five
Education

A Welsh Trust school existed in Machen as far back as 1674 which had twenty scholars. Such schools were set up through the efforts of two clergymen, Stephen Hughes and Thomas Gouge who were ejected from their livings because of their tolerant and nonconformist views. They raised money from many quarters in order to provide Welsh bibles bound with singing psalms which were sold in Wales at the printer's price of 4/2 a copy. Many were given away to the poor. After Gouge's death the schools gradually ceased.

Circulating Schools

The Welsh circulating schools were to follow founded by Griffith Jones of Llanddowror in the Teifi Valley. His system was to educate teams of teachers who then visited different areas staying for up to three months with the support of the local clergy, teaching children by day and their parents at night. Machen had a circulating school in 1740 with 62 pupils, and in 1764 a school was being held at Ysgubor Fach with 125 pupils. Dr William Price, the local eccentric and cremationist, attended a day school run by a Mr Gatwood in the early 1800s at Machen for three years from the age of ten. Local tradition has it that this school was in Pandy Lane.

The National Society archives record that in 1833 there were four day schools in Machen, containing 68 boys and 33 girls, seven of which were 'instructed at the expense of the Rector, all the rest at that of their parents.' There were also two Sunday schools, one connected with the Wesleyan Methodists with 80 children, and one run by the Baptists with 30 children.

The school at the Run

A letter in the Tredegar Estate archives written by the Rector, the Rev. Augustus Morgan mentions that a school was held in a cottage adjacent to the tinworks 'on the Monmouthshire side of the river'. This would indicate a house at the top of the Run, later lived in by a Mrs Bell which remains to this day. This school in 1847 was an appendage to the Machen Forge and Tin Works and was thought of by the Rector to be merely 'an infant school of which the principal object is to afford asylum for young children during working hours of those who are employed during the day'. The cottage belonged to Ysgubor Fach, tenanted by a George Powell, but owned by Lord Tredegar. Philip Woodruff who ran the tinworks wanted the cottage for his workers, and was prepared to build a school wherever Lord Tredegar offered Machen land in exchange.

The new school built by Philip Woodruff *c*. 1853 on the triangular piece of ground at Ffwrrwm, as Upper Machen was then known, later called the Church Room and now the Church Hall. The cost was about £70 and it was built by a Mr Williams who was also working on a renovation of the Ffwrrwm Ishta public house. The schoolroom was the property of Lord Tredegar, and under the control of the Rev. Augustus Morgan. The junior mixed school erected in 1872 can be seen in the bottom right-hand corner.

'My father who was born in 1889 told me there was a small school in the house at the top of the Run. His father sent him there when he was about three years old, and he paid a halfpenny a day. He did not go to the school in the Church Room because the family went to Siloam chapel, but later on he went to the school over the river. When it was time for him to leave, Mr Inkin signed his leaving certificate.' [EP]

'Our school was then a long low building right in the centre of the village (Church Room). The upper half was partitioned off for the older scholars, the lower half for the infants. The first class I attended was called the babies' class. We sat on small chairs around a long table, a coal fire was our heating in winter, a stout iron guard protecting it. We used a tray of sand and with a wooden stick we drew our pictures and letters. Then with a pale grey clay we modelled an apple for the A and so on. For counting we used the abacus. Two more classes were in the school, here we used slates and pencils instead of sand.' [DD]

Under the 1870 Education Act it was stipulated that elementary schools should be available for all children, and where they had not previously existed they were to be administered by a School Board, although attendance was not compulsory until 1880. This idea did not find favour with Augustus Morgan. At this time there was a school at Lower Machen which he had established in 1834, and the school in the church room built by Philip Woodruff.

Lower Machen School and school house early this century. This was referred to by Her Majesty's Inspector in 1847 as 'an extremely ornamental and commodious building with a comfortable house for the master and mistress'. The first headmaster, Francis Thompson, was also Parish Clerk and Overseer for many years. He died in 1899 aged 93, and is buried in Lower Machen churchyard. The curriculum shows great emphasis on religious instruction which was given at the beginning of each day. Writing, reading of scriptures, learning the catechism, reading history and geography, spelling, dictation, entering sums, mental arithmetic and learning of tables occupied the remaining time.

The Other School

The population was increasing, and since the parish extended over the mountain to the boundary with Risca, there were also many children there to be educated. The Rector built two more National schools (Church schools) one on a site adjacent to the River Rhymney now known as Glan-yr-Afon, and the other at Waun Fawr on the Risca side of Machen mountain. One of the houses in Green Row was allocated for the headmaster of the boys' and girls' school over the river, and another to the headmistress who was to share her accommodation with the governess of the Church Room Infants' School. The latter school was to be enlarged, so by 1873 there were four schools approved by the Board of Education functioning in the parish: Lower Machen School, Upper Machen Junior Mixed School (the old school), Upper Machen Infants' School (now the Church Room), Waun Fawr Mixed School (on the Risca side of the mountain).

There are few records regarding Waun Fawr school, but there was a sizeable chemical/tin-plate works and collieries at Risca employing a large number of people, and many children requiring education. As Risca Board schools were built later than the Machen schools, Waun Fawr was also catering for Risca children in the early 1870s. The building consisted of one long room only in which boys, girls and infants were taught by the schoolmaster and his daughter. Average attendance in its first year was 90. Numbers dropped when Risca schools were built, and the closing down of the chemical works in 1894 led to families leaving the area. It appears that Waun Fawr and Lower Machen schools closed around the turn of the century.

Group 3 at Machen Girls' School, pre-1908. The iron railings were made in Machen foundry and erected in 1893. Phillip Woodruff commented, 'Weight of iron hurdles round school 2 tons 17 cwts. 2 qtr. 14 lbs, cost including putting up £40. Inspected hole at back of school, not very much. Do not think it will ever affect the schools, [boys' and girls'] they are as safe as any house in the parish.' The building, however, was abandoned 13 years later as being unsafe!

The previous headmasters of the old school 'over the river' were firstly David Richards and then Edward Connor. Mr Connor was appointed by a School Board in 1880, and met a tragic death in 1899 when walking home to Machen after visiting a friend at Llandanglws farm. He slipped and fell near the quarry on to the railway line and died several hours later from exposure. He was succeeded by Mr Griffith Inkin.

An old account from the Scholastic Trading Company of Cardiff in 1873 states that 8-foot desks with slate rack and fitted with inkwells, made of pitch pine cost 34/- each, while 8-foot desks specially ordered with turn-down flaps for fixing on a gallery for infants cost 24/- each. A gallery consisted of desks arranged in shallow tiers so that infants could see, and be seen, easily. Exercise books cost 1/6 a dozen, pens and pencils were 9d a dozen, a gross of pen holders cost 1/6, and copies of the catechism were one old penny each.

Augustus Morgan died in 1875, and Phillip Woodruff became manager of the schools. The infant school log book records that there was 'a half day holiday for the children to attend the funeral of the Rev. Augustus Morgan, the promoter of the Machen Schools. They walked in procession to the parish church [St Michael's, Lower Machen].'

The accounts for 1876 show that the expenditure of £375 for these schools was met by education grants, subscriptions from landowners and voluntary rates. School pence of 2d, 3d, and 4d, dependent on size of family, was collected and allowed against salaries which amounted to £329, plus cleaning and coal which totalled £18.

Plaque erected to commemorate the enlargement of the infant school. This is placed at the gable end of the porch, facing the main road, which used to be the original entrance to the school.

The Board Schools

The schools became Board schools in 1880, and were visited yearly by the school inspector who would decide how much grant would be paid for attendance, and passes in the 'three Rs'. All children were allowed free schooling from August 1891 when collection of school pence ceased. By this time there was serious overcrowding in the infant school, and another room and cloak room were added. These were used for the first time on 23 October 1893. At the beginning of this century school attendance and illness were the main problems affecting children's education. Bad weather was detrimental to attendance because children were not well-shod nor warmly dressed. Heating in the schools was minimal, and an old school log book mentions that if they were too wet on arrrival it was necessary to send for a member of the School Board to give permission to close school for fear of them catching cold. Scarlet fever, which spread rapidly, was responsible for many deaths, and whooping cough, measles and chicken pox were common. Tuberculosis was not mentioned in the old log book, but was referred to by Mr Inkin in 1913, and was prevalent well into the 1950s. The poverty caused by the strike of 1926 led to some children being fed in school, but by 1934 cases of malnutrition were far less common. The County Medical Officer visiting the school commented on 'the splendid condition of the children from a physical and clothing standpoint'. However, there was still much unemployment in the area, and boots were distributed to children whose families were in need. At that time there were 90 children in school whose parents had been without work for a very long time.

Mr Inkin

Griffith David Inkin who was appointed headmaster of 'the old school' in 1899 at the relatively young age of 26, was a man who set high standards and expected his staff to do likewise. Great attention was paid to discipline, and respect, courtesy and good manners were instilled into all pupils under his charge. He was an avid exponent of the 'three Rs', and these subjects formed the backbone of the curriculum, although he was sufficiently flexible in his outlook to encourage important but less rigid subjects.

Official opening of the present junior mixed school on 11 January 1909 by Cllr. W.H. Davies, the senior representative of the managers, a well-known local dignitary. The school had actually been open since 26 August 1907 with Mr G.D. Inkin as headmaster. A temporary school, remembered by a few as a tin-sheet building was in use for a short time adjacent, whether as overspill or because the old building was unsafe is not clear.

Class of infants 1915. Back row: Miss E. Potter, Vernon Thomas, Kenneth Everson, Stanley Partridge, Bill Griffiths, Billy ?, Harold Beeston, Walter Rees, George Minty, Harold Everson, Jack Davies ('Shon'), Billy Banfield, Harold Llewellyn. Third row: Iris Jones, Annie Richards, Brenda Thomas, Irene Davies, Molly Harding, Mabel Graves, Ena Young, Margaret Beacham, Ivy Jenkins, Keziah Salathiel, Dolly Minty. Second row, Hugh Jones, Leslie Willetts, Sidney Everson, Bessie Everson, Eileen Harris, Gwyneth Everson, Audrey Rowlands, Ivy Jones, Agnes Jenkins, Mildred Richards, Norman Williams, Nancy Thomas. Front row: Garnon Willans, Ernest Thomas, Lyn Thomas, Ralph Green, Courtney Minty, Cyril Davies, Kenneth Harrington, Fred Harris, Tom Voyce, Hadyn Evans, Lyn Harding.

'At the age of seven years we were transferred to the big school as we called it, and by this time most of us could read quite well. When I was ready a new school had been built and this was very modern by the standards of those days. Particular stress was put on good handwriting. To assist us here we were issued with books with the Proverbs written in copperplate, and we copied these into the lines below. No little girls were without a pinafore at school, and all our teachers wore black sateen aprons.' [DD]

'My father was born in 1892 and went first to the infant school and then to the old school over the river. One day in playtime the rugby ball went flying over the iron railings and into the water. He and a friend chased it alongside the river, finally rescuing it by the Ffwrrwm Ishta pub. They took it back to school feeling very pleased with themselves for saving it, and also expecting praise for so doing. Their pleasure was short-lived. Mr Inkin gave them each three stripes for being late.

On another occasion, having been introduced to the stories of Robin Hood, he and his pals were playing in the Vedw and had made themselves bows and arrows. Hearing voices, they hid in the bushes and jumped out shouting appropriate words to find to their horror, Mr and Mrs Inkin surveying them. He smiled and congratulated them on their enterprise, commenting 'I am glad to know that you listened thoroughly to the story'. When my Dad was in his eighties we went for a picnic in the Wye Valley, and he recited O, Sylvan Wye... by Wordsworth. I asked him how he came to know it, and he replied, 'Oh, Inkin taught us that'. Whenever the hunt was out we boys would follow it for miles. I did this one lunch time, got back late to school, and Mr Inkin was waiting. All he said was 'Hounds?', and that was it. I knew what to expect.' [EJC]

Standard IV, 1928. From left to right, back row: Victor Perkins, Raymond Johns, Jackie Jones, Ron Davies, Vivian Escott, Ralph Minty, Emlyn Jones, Ken Llewellyn, Glyn Organ. Second row: Alma Gimblett, Marie Tatlow, Joan Matthews, Doris Green, Muriel Pope, Florence Griffiths, Beryl Matthews, Hilda Partridge, Olga Thomas, Nancy Rogers, Mr Inkin. Third row: -?-, Lorna Jones, Gwen Cousins, Dilys Buckley, Megan Jones, Stella Smith, Gwyneth Price, Phyllis Credgington, Dorothy Willetts, Linda Harris. Fourth row: Doug Evans, David Rees, Neville Ellis, ? Beecham, Ewart Martin, John Thomas, Percy Dowdeswell. Bottom row: John Prince, Arthur Rogers, Ray Bristow.

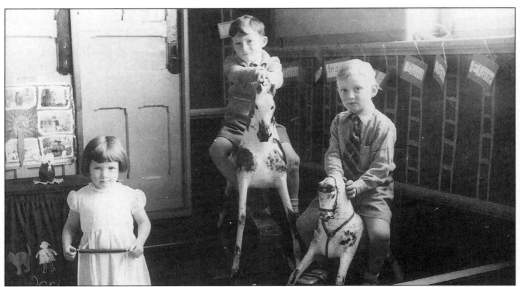

Dobbin, the well-remembered rocking-horse who greeted newcomers to the infant school, with Iris Moses, Phillip Wade and Bill Merchant.

'I always remember Miss Henney. She used to delight to tell you stories, and she was good at it. She told us about the Water Babies and the chimney sweep. She used to have a picture of it in the third class of the infants.' [VR]

'One day, in the playground at the new school, Mr Inkin came up to a group of us and asked, 'Which direction is north from here?' Fred Brown said, 'Over there, sir, by Corn Roberts's farm'. He was told 'Your geography is correct, but it is Cornelius Roberts, and to you, it is Mr Roberts'. Wham, wham, wham. When Fred passed the scholarship he was told at the Grammar School that Machen boys were two years ahead in their maths.' [LH]

'We always had a concert for St David's Day, and I often had to sing. Mr Inkin would come into the class and beckon me to go with him. I used to wonder what I had done wrong, then he would give me a song and if I didn't know it, he would sit down at the piano and play it over for me to learn. He was a very good pianist and usually played for morning assembly.' [CC]

'He was a fine headmaster, very strict and none of us was any the worse for it. One day I was on the road and passed by the two Misses Righton, and Mr Inkin was further up the street. Next day in school he had me in his office. 'You went for a walk yesterday, didn't you?' 'Yes, sir'. 'You passed two ladies, didn't you?'. 'Yes, sir'. 'You did not raise your hat to them.' 'No, sir.' 'Three strokes!' [WH]

'We used to play a game in school called 'Longy Della'. All but two of us would get against the one wall of the playground and one of those was always Mr Llewellyn, the teacher. He would come down and join us, and he and one of the bigger boys would stay in the centre. We would all start shouting 'Longy Della', and start rushing across the playground. They would try to catch two or three, and then there were four or five in the middle. Then we would start again until the last was caught, and he was the hero of the day.' [AR] This game was a great proving ground for many a Machen rugby player.

'He was certainly a personality as I know to my cost. One night we were playing on the swings in the rec, and when Mr Dick Trew, the caretaker, blew his whistle you were expected to file out. A gang of us, mostly Adullam boys, filed out and just when we got to the entrance, we doubled back and went on the swings. We did this several times, laughing and joking. Mr Trew tried to get us out, and suddenly the laughter stopped, and I saw Ossie Willetts glance across the river and there was Mr Inkin standing on his doorstep looking at us. We slunk away and I, personally, had a very restless night. We went to school the next day and stood together in assembly, Ossie, Ernie Everson and the rest of the gang and waited. I breathed a sigh of relief as he stood down from the platform and piano, and I thought we had got away with it. Then he walked straight across to us and said 'Go down the steps!' So we lined up outside his door, seven of us. He went about his business of organising morning school, and looking back on it, he did it deliberately. We were sweating blood. He came down, left his door open, went to his inner cupboard and we could see him testing his canes. One of us, his nerve broke, and he said, 'I told them to come away, Mr Inkin.' He replied, 'Right, I'll start with YOU.' [MH]

'There were a lot of children where I lived in Chatham, and Mr Inkin lived up the road. He would be waiting for us with a whistle, and we would all walk together up the road in front of him. Any messing about, and the whistle would go!' [DV]

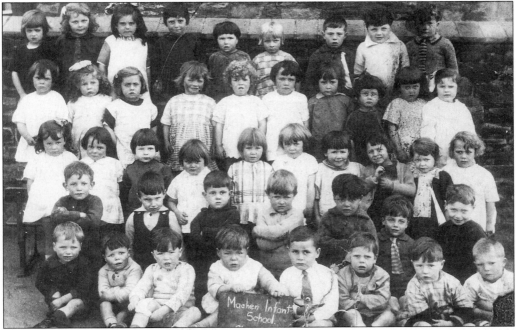

Infant class, 1928. Back row: Connie Hartley, -?-, Iris Edmunds, Daphne Hicks, Hilda Matthews, Arthur Minty, Graham Davies, -?-. Second row: -?-, Eileen Dickinson, Dorothy Credgington, -?-, Gaynor Davies, Barbara Davey, Rita Williams, Maisie Gregory, Patti Hill, -?-. Third row: -?-, Nancy Rowlands, Megan Morgan, Joy Partridge, Jean Evans, -?-, Dorothy Rees, Dorothy Jones, Sadie Davies, Lorraine Jones. Fourth row: Alec Rees, Trevor Jones, Milwyn Moses, Garfield Harrington, Victor Pope, -?-, -?-. Front row: Neville Ellis, John Davies, Gwyn Vines, Percy Heath, Graham Barnard, Ken Holland, -?-, John Davies.

'Mr Llewellyn always used to give us a general knowledge test on a Friday afternoon, and the one that got the most answers right had a lovely big bar of chocolate.' [DG]

'It always seemed to me that Mr Llewellyn taught you in a quiet gentle sort of way. He was very good on geography, and we would make relief maps with pulped newspapers. We did Monmouthshire and Spain, because it was the time of the Civil War [1936-39], I suppose.' [HE]

The School Museum

'The punishment for talking during lessons never varied, we were dismissed from the classroom to stand in the hall. This could be very boring, had it not been for our museum which was a big bookcase containing amongst other treasures, some bird's eggs. Holding pride of place in the centre was an ostrich egg.' [DD]

'The museum was a book case on top, with a cupboard below with glass doors which were kept locked. There was a huge coconut with a segment taken out of it and one of the hoofs of 'Sir Briggs', the horse that had carried Captain Godfrey Morgan, later 2nd Baron Tredegar, into battle at the Charge of the Light Brigade in 1854. Miss Gimblett used to read the whole poem to us with accompanying dramatic gestures. I still remember very clearly that she took us one summer day for a nature walk to Pentwyn pit and told us to lie down in the grass, close our eyes, listen to the birds, smell the flowers, and store up memories for when we were old. In the main hall on the east wall, there was a sort of Highway Code on how to be a good Christian. The first item was 'Cleanliness is next to Godliness'. Since Mam was always exhorting us to wash behind our ears before going to chapel, it always seemed to me that it ought to be the other way round.' [EJC]

Top infants, 1933. Back row: -?-, Gertie Williams, Desmond Davies, Gwyn Vines, Mervyn Williams, Percy Heath, -?-, Celia Howells, Wilfred Hawkins. Second row: Elunid Davies, -?-, Ernie Jones, Maurice Sanders, Raymond Jones, Peter Barnard, John Davies, Dorothy Purnell, -?-. Third row: Joy Partridge, Ivy Perkins, Les Rowles, Billy Dickinson, Clive Coleman, Pam Williams, Doug Everson, Megan Davey, Patti Hill. Front row: Dorothy Davies, Cliff Farmer, Sadie Davies, Eunice Jones, Doreen Hucker, Neville Ellis, Joyce Hill, Ralph Jones.

School group, 1937-38. From left to right, back row: Mr Spinks, Dennis Richards, Roy Bodrell, Dennis Hartley, Arthur Luke, Eddie Watkins, Dennis Perrott, Reggie Button, Eric Bundy, Artie Williams. Second row: Lorraine Watson, Iris Llewellyn, Doreen Phipps, Sadie Nicholas, Pat Perry, Val Rogers, Kathleen Jones, Mavis Hartley, Edwina Everson, Pattie Spinks. Third row: Noeline Stephen, Iris Rowlands, Margaret Jones, Joan Gray, Hazel Spargo, Ann Rees, Maureen Morris, Beryl Walley, Elaine Davies. Front row: Frank Norman, Roy Harris, Mickie Fitzgerald, Graham Skuse, Dennis Harper, Aubrey Askey, Graham Jones, Bee Stephen.

School group, c. 1940. Back row: Barbara George, Barbara Beacham, Lynette Passmore, Fay Beacham, Vaile Woosnam, Jane Beeston, Middle Row, Ken Davies, Emrys Podmore, Lawrence Norris, Gwyn Jones, Nesta Price, Betty Jones, Front Row, Kathleen Norris, Margaret Minty, Joyce Harris, Doreen Butler, David Phillips, Mavis Jones.

Junior school group, 1954. Back row: Tony Richards, Geoffrey Kendall, Brian Young, Douglas Willetts, John Anthony, John Beeston, Phillip Morris, Raymond Minty, Robin Bayliss, Colin Richards. Second row: Brian Greenhaf, Susan Voyce, Anita Grocutt, Crystal Rowe, Jean Roderick, Stephanie Bartlemore, Betty Maddocks, Jane Whittington, Bill Thompson. Front row: Valerie Jones, Pauline Joseph, Gloria Fox, Lynne Beavis, Christine Sullivan, Gillian Were, Gillian Bull, Rene Roger, Doreen Shattock, Christine Secombe.

It is remarkable that memories of Griffith Inkin are so vivid for so many people. He served the community in many ways, and was held in great respect by all. He was succeeded by Mr T.A. Bateman who died following an appendicitis operation two years later in 1937. Several members of staff were with the school for many years, notably Mr J.T. Spinks who joined the staff in 1919 and became headmaster in 1937. Mr Emrys Llewellyn commenced in 1922, and took over as acting headmaster when Mr Spinks joined HM Forces in the Second World War. Miss Alma Gimblett was one of the first teachers when the present school opened in 1907. Mrs Enid Harrington was another long-serving and respected teacher who also acted as head teacher in 1969 and 1973-74.

Head Teachers

G.D. Inkin (1907-1935), T.A. Bateman (1935-1937), J.T. Spinks (1937-1954), J.H. Broom (1955-1960), W.A. Smith (1960-1966) G. Evans (1966-1969), W.R. Edmunds (1970-1973), P.G. Jones (1974-1993), Miss L. Hunter (1993-)

Six
Religion

At the turn of the century there were seven centres of worship in Machen, namely the parish church of St Michael's at Lower Machen, the church of St John's in Upper Machen, together with two Baptist chapels, two Wesleyan, and a Congregational chapel. To this was to be added the Pentecostal church founded in 1917. In common with many other communities, the number has now been greatly reduced. The churches remain, together with Ebenezer Baptist chapel and Emmanuel Pentecostal, with the addition of a daughter-church group of St Peter which worships at the Graig-y-Rhacca junior school, part of Machen parish.

The Baptists

The early Baptists are recorded as worshipping from 1787 to 1802 in the area of Ysgubor Fach farm. They later moved down to the village and rented a site in 1820 from David and William Thomas who were farmers and victuallers, David at The Tredegar Arms and William at The Ffwrrwm Ishta. They met in the home of a William Jenkins before building a chapel in 1820, which date is confirmed in the 1851 religious census. This was fully incorporated into the Baptist Union by 1829. Whether it was adjacent to the Siloam that was built eight years later is not clear, but since the census states that Siloam was erected in 1820 it would indicate it was possibly on the same site.

Siloam chapel (1837-1977).
Situated on Commercial Road, it was built in 1837 on ground given by a Mrs Evans for a chapel to be used for worship 'as long as there is a stone in the Rhymney River' (the wording in the original deed). There is little doubt that it was much loved and well-attended. The census reports that there was space for 523 people, and that the average attendance for the previous year at morning, afternoon and evening worship was 420. The chapel had a good-sized vestry building and cottage adjacent, possibly the buildings used originally. It also had a baptistery which was a green-tiled tank sunk into the floor.

Siloam, the end of an era. Prior to 1884 services were in Welsh, English being introduced by John Morgan who came from Llanwenarth, Abergavenny. At the time of the great religious revival in 1904 it was an integral part of all religious life. A social centre was opened in 1937 which enabled its members to participate in various crafts including leatherwork, woodwork, needlework, cookery and art. This was carried on in the room above the vestry, which had also been a billiard room. The vestry itself had a small library, housed in high, glass-fronted cupboards which some older inhabitants say came from the old junior school. The main chapel was closed some years prior to its eventual demolition in 1977, although services continued to be held in the vestry. In 1995 the site of the chapel was re-designated a parking area. The vestry and cottage remain, and possible renovation for community use is currently being considered. The pastor for 51 years from 1921 was the Rev. Daniel Hughes (known as the 'sledge-hammer parson' since he had used one to break down the door of a chapel at Pontypool which was locked against him). He was a man of many parts, a lecturer for the WEA (Workers Education Association), member of the Monmouthshire County Council, Chairman of Bedwas and Machen Urban District Council, Governor of Bassaleg Secondary School, and was adopted as a Labour Parliamentary Candidate for the Monmouth constituency. He was well-known on both sides of the Atlantic and published an English-Welsh hymn book including many of his own compositions.

'Siloam was a four-square building with rectangular windows of clear glass, a gallery on three sides, varnished pine seats throughout, and on the white wall behind the large central pulpit in bold characters of blue and gold, the words 'God is Love', all very plain and simple. The singing was splendid, especially at the evening service, when the men in the choir in the gallery above, mostly miners and railwaymen, gave full voice to *Jesu, Lover of my Soul* and *All Hail the power of Jesus' name*. The Sunday school hymns tended to be sentimental. Some were of questionable validity for small children, while others such as *Jesus wants me for a Sunbeam* were quite ridiculous from the lips of a twelve-year-old boy who was pulling the hair of the girl in front of him.' [AJ]

'Daniel Hughes was a marvellous orator, and I always felt he should have been an actor at Stratford-upon-Avon. I always remember one sermon 'And there was a garden', then he went on about the garden of Gethsemane. We used to call him Danny Boy.' [LR]

'One of his best lectures was on Jerome K. Jerome's *Three Men in a Boat*, and another was on *A Christmas Carol*. He had two cottages at Penallt near Monmouth, and he would invite members of the congregation there for a day out. One was called 'The Cabin' and the other was 'The Nook'. He would let down-and-outs stay in one, and he never worried about money.' [LB]

Ebenezer Baptist chapel, Wyndham Street still stands today and is in regular use. It was built in 1884 for a breakaway group which left Siloam in 1883 with its Pastor, the Rev. D. Lloyd, who then decided to leave them for the business world. Its first minister was the Rev. Isaac Moses who served for thirty-two years until 1916 when he was presented with an illuminated address, together with a purse of gold in appreciation of his labours. In the early years the Moses family were prominent in its affairs, John, Jacob and Abraham holding office as secretary, treasurer and precenter. One of their last lay ministers was Dai Moses. It was bought by the Chapel Trustees for £67. 10s 0d in 1925 at the Tredegar Estate sale in the Church Room.

The ordination service for the Rev. Trevor Rees at Ebenezer Baptist chapel, 1958. From left to right: Mr W.J. Martin, Rev. T. Rees, Rev. E. Roberts, Mr R.O. Rees and Mr A.T. Elliott.

Ebenezer

'There was a wonderful spirit of endeavour with all the Ebenezer people. I remember being told how, after raising the money, the men took over and built it. Some of them had a trade: one was a mason and builder, Walter Rosser, and he did a lot of the work, including the mouldings on the ceiling in the vestry. They would go straight there from work, the wives would take their dinner up, and they would eat and get on with the building. They used a lot of the yellow bricks from the old brickworks opposite Colliers Row.' [IR]

The Congregationalists (Independent)

Dr Thomas Rees' *History of Protestant Nonconformity in Wales* mentions a following of Congregationalists in Machen as far back as 1772. At that time they were known as 'Independents'. Their chapel was built in 1846 on the site of Rose Cottages, Church Street, and the 1851 census states that the building was near the foundry which was adjacent to Machen station. At that time the deacon was Evan Jones, who was a dyer at the Pandy Mill, and the attendance on census day was over 300, spread over morning, afternoon 'school' and evening service.

ADULLAM CHAPEL (1860-1970). Adullam cost £608 to build and stood at the top of Lewis Street. The English Congregational Union contributed £100, and the Rev. T.L. Jones was the minister. The chapel and some adjoining houses were sold for £100 at the Tredegar Estate sale in 1925. The Hicks family who worked in the tin-plate works for generations were founder members and deacons of the chapel. Mr G.D. Inkin was also a deacon (and organist) as was Tom Harding, the local painter and decorator.

Adullam chapel anniversary, 1911.

'I always had a new suit for the chapel anniversary. It was the same every year, navy blue, and that's probably why I have never had a navy blue suit since. One Sunday, Dennis Harper, Graham Lewis and myself were sitting up in the gallery close to the organ. We were fed up with the sermon and decided to creep along behind it. The preacher looked up at us, and made some remark about getting back to our places, but what was worse, Mr Inkin sitting in the front downstairs slowly turned round and just looked up at us. We knew he had seen us.' [HE]

'Tom Harding loved his hymns and, if it was a particular favourite, he would start singing the last verse again and off everyone would go with added fervour. Twice was not always sufficient: it could go into yet another repeat.' [EJC]

73

The Wesleyans

The Wesleyan Methodists had three chapels in Machen, two in Chatham, and one on Chapel Hill. The Welsh Methodist chapel, Capel Uchaf, was situated, appropriately, on Chapel Hill, and known as Wesley buildings. It was built in 1831, but has been used as a private dwelling for many years. Although the religious census records it had space for 252 worshippers, its average attendance was 120, which covered morning worshippers and scholars, and the evening congregation. It was sold in the 1920 Tredegar Estate sale.

The second Welsh chapel is referred to in the census as Capel y Groes, Calvinistic Methodist. This was situated on the main road, near the Reading Room. It was erected in 1843 and had an attendance of about 100, including 30 scholars. There does not appear to be any more information about these two chapels, and Graham Beeston in *Bedwas and Machen, Past and Present* suggests they ceased to function as the Welsh language started to disappear towards the end of the nineteenth century.

Mr Beeston states that his great-grandfather Joseph Beeston, a stone mason, organised services in a barn at Ysgubor Fach on behalf of the English Methodist Society in 1825. He then progressed to having services in a club room belonging to a public house which had lost its licence. This was offered to him by the Rector, the Rev. Augustus Morgan, who assisted in making the room suitable on the understanding that the timing of services did not clash with those of the parish church since the Methodists were good attenders there and Joseph was choirmaster to the church choir. The Wesleyan Methodist magazine of 1901 mentions that Joseph Beeston worked on the Tredegar Estate until his death, and that the public house lost its licence when the Rector made it into cottages. One also learns that the two men had a high regard for each other, and that Machen was the only village in the Risca circuit where John Wesley was known to have preached (1741).

Lower Machen forge and the cottages adjoining belonged to the Tredegar Estate, and Joseph Beeston was living there at the time of the 1841 census. The Beeston family have been there ever since. Bert Beeston, a descendant, told Fred Hando in 1961 that the cottages were originally The Rising Sun and a posting house. Marjorie Jones, now in her nineties, who has lived there all her life, was told by her mother that there was a large club room above with a stone staircase leading from below. This was most likely the Methodists' earlier meeting place.

The Committee on Education Enquiry of 1833 mentions the existence of a Sunday school connected with the Wesleyans consisting of 80 scholars, while the Upper Machen Infant School log book records that the Wesleyan Sunday school celebrated its centenary in the Church Room in 1880.

The 1851 census stated that Joseph Beeston and George Young were the preachers in Ebenezer Wesleyan erected that year, which had space for 218 people. One assumes the name must have been changed before 1884, when the Ebenezer Baptist chapel was built, since it is unlikely there would be two chapels of the same name in the village.

Four generations of the Beeston family in the 1880s outside Forge cottages, Lower Machen.

The English Wesleyan chapel at the bottom of Crown Street (Llanarth Street). Built at a cost of £600, it was demolished in the 1970s for housing.

'There was always a nice crowd there, and we used to go to Sunday school and for trips. When I was older I used to help Fred Brown when he took over the office. I had a class of boys when I was about 17, and often used to take the service for Fred if he could not come. I was President of the Sisterhood for over 20 years. Once a year we would get in contact with the other chapels, and they came from Bedwas, Caerphilly and Trethomas. We had a service and then we went down the Pandy fields until about 6 o'clock, then we had our tea. We would have races, skipping and running, and it was always lovely weather. You could always be sure of the weather in those days. Then we came back and we would have a special speaker. We had George Thomas [now Lord Tonypandy] one time, and I was by the pulpit with him. After the other chapels closed, a friend asked me to go to church with her, and that's what I did. It wouldn't be a Sunday without going to a place of worship. I have always gone.' [DV]

Emmanuel Pentecostal church

Emmanuel Pentecostal church. This church began when cottage meetings were held in various parts of the village. Mr Sidney Mercy, known as 'Father Mercy' from Cross Keys, was a retailer who walked over the mountain to Machen carrying a supply of boots which he sold on a credit basis. It was the beginning of the First World War, money was scarce and his customers repaid him at the rate of six pence a week. He was a strong believer in the second coming of Christ, and one of his first meetings was held in the home of Thomas Early at Ty-Gwyn above the railway line at The Royal Oak. Another staunch adherent was Edward Thomas of Nantygleisiad Cottage, White Hart, who later became a senior deacon and trustee, opening his home for meetings. By 1917 the 'second comers' as they were now known, were using the ground floor of a house in Commercial Road for their meetings. This house later became William Hicks' butcher's shop, and in more recent times, the Spar Stores. The house and Gospel Hall were sold in 1925 for £115 to J. Meyrick.

In 1926 it was decided to move to Forge Road. Under the pastorate of Arthur Thomas, son of Edward of Nantygleisiad, a timber-framed building clad with corrugated sheets was completed by Tommy Davies, the local carpenter and undertaker. It accommodated 120 people, with vestry and large baptismal pool.

In 1966, after a baptismal service, it was found on going to empty the tank the next day, that the pool was empty. The water had escaped under the floor boards. Later that year during a crowded service the whole congregation slowly dropped about eighteen inches. The joists had rotted as a result the seepage of water, and the floor had collapsed. Undaunted, rebuilding commenced in 1967, and was completed and paid for when it was opened in March 1968. Emmanuel was founded in the years of great unemployment and depression, and a number of families from the church moved to the Midlands to obtain work. In spite of low wages, the members shared their money amongst those without work and gave a tenth of their income (a tithe) to the church. Arthur Thomas remained Pastor for over forty years. He took no pay, so that considerable sums of money were given to those in need or to establish new churches at home and overseas. Edward Watkins, the grandson of Edward Thomas of Nantygleisiad, took over the pastorate, retiring in 1993, to be succeeded by Dr Edmund Aubrey, both of whom continued the pattern of being self-supporting by following their chosen professions.

St John's church

This church was built in 1855 in the time of the Rev. Augustus Morgan. There was a need for another church because of the rapidly increasing population who would have found the chapels more convenient than the parish church in Lower Machen which was some distance away.

The Rector remarked in his address at the laying of the foundation stone, that he was 'fully aware of the rapid increase in the population' and was solicitous for the welfare of 'those persons, who from age, infirmity or other causes, had been unable to go to Lower Machen.' The list of subscribers to the building fund was headed with a gift of £400 from Edward Buller, who had leased Machen colliery, Sir Charles Morgan gave the land, and other contributions came from the tin-plate works, the Rumney Railway, the Monmouthshire Canal Company and various members of the Morgan family.

The *Monmouthshire Merlin* reports that the laying of the foundation stone on 22 June 1854 was very well-attended, and the Rector had 'engaged one of Mr Phillip's omnibuses to bring a goodly party of ladies and gentlemen from Newport'. Tents were erected on the grounds, and the Machen Band was in attendance together with the National school children. The ceremony was carried out by Mrs Augustus Morgan who, on being presented with a richly-chased silver trowel with an appropriate inscription, buried beneath the stone a bottle containing current coins of the realm, and two poems, one in Welsh and one in English. The former was composed by Mr William Jones, churchwarden, who was the manager of the fulling mill at the Pandy, the latter poet remaining anonymous. Although building did not commence until June 1854, it was completed for opening on 13 September 1855.

The paper continues: 'The gentry and their ladies were treated to an excellent cold lunch, a feature of which was the wine and also a large supply of finest strawberries placed on the tables by Mr W. Power, gardener at Tredegar Park. In the other tent, with a commendable consideration for the working classes who were permitted by their employers, Messrs Buller, Woodruff and Russell, three masters of the neighbourhood, to enjoy the day as a holiday, was provided a substantial treat of roast beef, cheese, bread and *cwrw da* which was partaken of with right good appetite by the workers of the wealth of the district. The school children of Upper and Lower Machen, who had formed a pleasing group in front of the church carrying gay banners with mottoes, were given tea and cakes in the Infants' Schoolroom.'

Church Christmas pantomime.

The first Clerk for the English services and caretaker was William Cook, whose four-year old son was the first to be buried in the new churchyard in May 1856, having fallen from the roof when the weathercock was installed. Members of the Cook family remained as caretakers, and in some cases, as organists, well into this century. The last member of the family to carry out this office was Ray Cook, who died in 1993.

The building has not had any structural alterations since its dedication. In 1919 the stained glass window above the altar was donated by Mrs S.L. Wade of the Volland in memory of her father W.R. Lloyd who had been People's Warden for forty years. She also had the old glass recut and placed in the two smaller chancel windows. This century, renovation works have been carried out at the time of the centenary in 1955, and more recently in 1990-94.

A robed choir was formed in 1923-24, during the ministry of the Rev. A.G.A. Picton MC, and the appointed choirmaster was Mr Jack Morley. Numerous anthems would be sung at festivals such as Easter, when *Olivet to Calvary* or *Messiah* would be the great favourites. The organ then was a blower-type, which necessitated someone seated at the side to continually pump. This was replaced by the present organ in 1935, which was bought from Picton Castle, West Wales.

St Michael's church

St Michael's, Lower Machen. The present building, which is the parish church, dates from the eleventh century, when it was given together with Bassaleg and Bedwas and several other chapelries to the Abbey of Glastonbury. In 1535 it was established as a separate rectory, and in 1710 the patronage passed to the Morgan family, who are commemorated on the fine hatchments to be seen on its interior walls. The church has a Morgan chapel with many monuments to the various members buried there.

A major renovation took place in 1901, which included restoration of the tower and removal of the gallery at the west end. The cost of repairs was defrayed by Lord Tredegar, but a 'hot air heating' system was paid for by the parishioners.

There was originally a peal of six bells cast in 1768, by Thomas Bailey, a bell founder from Bridgewater, Somerset, although the fourth bell needed recasting in 1856. In 1912 the bell frame was in such a ruinous state that it was decided to replace the wood with an iron and steel frame, a new chiming apparatus and to increase the peal from six to eight bells. The cost of this scheme was £350. 11s 0d. The parish registers commence in 1686 for marriages, 1670 and 1671 for christenings and burials. There are parish records dealing with the expenditure of elected parish officers in connection with the working of the Poor Law, and the work of the Petty Constables and Surveyors of the Highways from 1734 to 1826.

Since 1968 St Michael's has been the venue for a prestigious music festival held annually, at which many internationally famous artists perform.

Passion play at St Michael's church, 1950s. From left to right, back row: Gwilym Evans, Beatrice Davies, Mostyn Bennett, -?-, -?-, Betty Deacon, Bernard Spooner, John Matthews, Eileen George, Malcolm Thomas.

Church and chapel social life

Attendance at Sunday and weekday services was an accepted part of life, but so were the social events which were organised by its followers. The Church ran many activities which catered for its members, the Mothers' Union, Girls' Friendly Society and Church Men's Guild. The Church Room included a billiard room which was very popular. This was altered eventually to make way for the present stage. The Lower Machen schoolroom was used for dances and rummage sales and after the Second World War, the WI would meet for canning sessions to preserve fruit, which was still a scarce commodity in austere post-war Britain. Anniversaries, concerts, pantomimes, religious drama, tea parties and trips to the seaside were high points in village life. The chapel anniversaries were occasions when the young would perform a 'party piece' with a small reward, often a coin or gift presented in a small hand-sewn 'anniversary bag'. It was the time for new dresses, sometimes of velvet made up at the Monkey House, and for hats swathed in net and ribbons to catch the eye. When a chapel had its anniversary, the other chapels would often close so that everyone could join together.

Ebenezer social gathering, 1950s. Among those pictured are: Granville Jones, Ted Brown, William Martin, Eva May Jones, Sidney Davies, Reg. Rees, Blodwen Martin, Mrs Olwen Davies (née Rees), Eldon Gadd, Bronwen Moses, Dorothy Price, Rosanna Phillips, Prudence Powell, Rev. D.G. Thomas, Mrs Turner, Mrs D. Jones, Mrs D. Evans, Mrs Elliott, Mrs Voyce, Mrs R. Price, Mrs R. Rees, Mrs E. Haskins, Mrs S. Davies, Mrs S. Price, Mrs A. Rosser, Mrs D. Jones, Mr D. Moses, Mrs D.J. Thomas, Miss Gladys Vines.

High Days and Holidays

Whitsun Monday was the 'Parade Day' when we did a lap of the village, each Sunday school behind its own banner, the silver band in front playing as they sang *Marching to Zion*, and then it was back for tea, and what a tea it was. The tables were loaded with food, while our mothers in starched white aprons bustled to and fro, carrying huge tea pots. Then followed sports, and a chance to clear up any leftovers from tea. When we went on the best treat of all to the Lighthouse [at St Brides] some seven miles away, we used to set out early in horse-traps and brakes, carrying large bags of food. When the procession of traps got to Machen Fach, the hill was too steep for the horses, and everyone had to get out except the elderly. On the return journey, it was the reverse, everyone walked down the hill to save straining the animals. How we enjoyed ourselves on that day, we caught crabs under the rocks and climbed the circular stairs at the Lighthouse.' [DD]

'The only holidays we used to have up until I was sixteen [1926], was when we went with the chapel to Barry. We had a coach then. Horace Morgan from Caerphilly took us and we used to have to walk up Nantgarw Hill because there was no strength in those old coaches.' We used to go camping, make a tent up in the wood with old sticks, ferns and things like that and take potatoes from home and we'd cook them. As soon as they were black they were done!' [VT]

'Dick Heath used to clean his coal lorry, put trestles in it, and take us down to the Lighthouse at St Brides. There was a swimming pool there where they used to baptise people.' [VR]

'When we knew we were going down 'the Moors' we used to go up to Dick Heath's shed at the top of Crown Street and sweep out his coal lorry. He fitted struts and a canvas top and put trestles in it. The only attractions there were one or two stalls, a small playground with swings and a see-saw, and a bathing pool. This pool was sometimes used for conducting open-air baptisms. One day when I was about nine, and in a push chair because I'd had an accident, I was baptised in the pool by Pastor Jeffries. He probably thought he was doing me good!' They changed the water regularly – every high tide.' [RD]

'The church outing usually went to Barry Island, and I always remember looking for the peacock cut out in the privet hedge in Forge Lane, and some of the larger ladies tucking their dresses in their knickers when they went paddling.' [BP]

'When we went by coach, you really got excited if it was a Cridlands coach, because they were really up-market. They had an open top and solid tyres. We always went to The Merry Friar on the sea front, and everyone sat at long trestle-tables. The treat was two pieces of cake, a sultana cake, and a piece of what we called 'sawdust cake', mine usually had jam and cream in it.' [AR]

'I remember one time when my wife and son went on the Sunday school outing to Barry, I enquired of my neighbour what time they would be returning. She considered carefully and replied 'Well, Mr Davies, they went off fairly good this morning, so they ought to be back fairly middling.' [LD]

'From Siloam, at Whitsun, we used to go the Six o'clock Field to enjoy a magnificent spread laid out on trestle tables. Afterwards, we had races and games, but most of us boys went to catch bull-heads in Draethen brook.' [EJC]

Adullam Chapel Sisterhood, 1930s.

Siloam members on an outing to Taf Fechan reservoir, early 1930s. The group includes: Alf
Cage, Ted James, Marjorie Kellow, Bob Holland, John Coleman, Eli Coleman, Coral Coleman,
Mrs Cage, Mrs Beach, Reg Minty, Cyril Davies, Lloyd Harris, Hughie Kellow, Mrs 'Brom'
Davies, Maggie Kellow, Marie Kellow, Bob Green, Clarice Rodway, Eva May Jones, Alma
Gimblett, B. Rodway, Rene Richards, Lillibel Holland, Will 'Brom' Davies.

Mother's race at the church fête on the Recreation Ground, 1950s. Note the Reading Room before alterations and top of picture, the Vedw House.

Ebenezer Sisterhood outing, 1950s. From left to right: Mrs D. Price. Mrs L. Bennett, Mrs E.M. Jones, Mrs F. Howard, Mrs A. Rosser, Mrs I. Rees, Mr Ted Lloyd (driver), -?-, Mrs J. Richards, Mrs L. Askey, Mrs E. Rees, Mrs p. Powell, Mrs C. Jones.

Seven

Wartime

The dedication of Machen War Memorial by Lord Tredegar on 12 February 1921. The War Memorial sited below St John's church is a silver grey Celtic cross of Cornish granite inscribed with the names of those who gave their lives in the two World Wars: 1914-1918 and 1939-1945. The 'war to end all wars' as the First World War was known, claimed 29 men and the second conflict 19.

When unveiling the memorial, Lord Tredegar reminded those present that he himself was a Machen boy, and if there was any memorial that he would like to attend, it was that of the neighbours among whom he had spent such a happy boyhood. He said also that 230 of the village population had joined up. The Rev. A.G.A. Picton who conducted the service had himself been decorated with the Military Cross during the war.

By 1915 the village was raising money to buy gifts for servicemen when they came home on leave. Football matches, concerts and regular house-to-house collections were organised and presentations were made in Siloam and Adullam chapels, or in the Church Room by various local people. Shaving outfits, pocket watches, cigarette cases and walking sticks were chosen by the men themselves, although some declined a presentation; possibly the terrible slaughter witnessed by many in the trenches influenced this decision. Many who returned did not wish to talk, or be reminded of what had gone on in France and elsewhere.

Waiting to welcome home troops from the First World War in the Church field, now part of the churchyard but, at one time, Machen's football field.

'I was about eight years old when the Armistice was signed on the 11 November 1918. All we schoolchildren went round every street, Chatham, White Hart, everywhere, the whole lot of us banging saucepans, kettles and pans with sticks.' [LR]

The village postmaster, William Ebrill Edwards, composed, printed and published several patriotic songs. Amongst these were *My Little Dug-out*, *Cheer the Boys in Khaki* and *When the Boys Return* on sale at 6d per copy in the Music Stores (the old Post Office).

Belgian refugees

Madam Shore and her two daughters, Belgian refugees, lived at 81 Commercial Road where they stayed for three years. The younger daughter attended Machen School, and when Mr Inkin saw that she was in need of spectacles he duly had them provided. Notice the Belgian flag suspended over the road, as well as the Union Jacks in the windows.

Machen was also involved with the Belgian Relief Fund which commenced in January 1915 to give shelter to 250,000 Belgian refugees during the war. Regular village collections were made together with grants received from a central committee in Newport, and Machen workmen in Risca colliery made generous donations which enabled shelter to be given to three families. The Co-op gave free bread and cake for one month after arrival, coal was bought, rooms offered and houses eventually rented, while furniture, linen and utensils were donated. Two families were resident for eighteen months before returning to London. The third family is pictured above.

Horse Power

'My brother Bayliss, was a blacksmith, and served in France. After the war, a huge stallion, over 17 hands high, was brought to him to be shod. No one else would attempt it, but he was marvellous with horses and had no trouble at all. He said to me afterwards that it was easy compared to shoeing horses and mules with shells and bullets exploding all around you.' [MJ]

'At the beginning of the war in 1914 there were some 200 men working at Pentwyn pit and so many of them went to the front together with their horses that it had to close. It makes one realise how vital horse-power was at that time.' [JT]

The 'welcome home' meal being prepared in Machen School, 1919, with Mrs Cornelius Roberts, third from left. Machen had a British Legion branch when war was declared in 1939. This had been formed in 1932 and originally met in the old bakehouse at the back of the Co-op shop, paying a rental of 5/- per week. The Legion Hall there was shared with the ARP (Air Raid Precautions) and the St John Ambulance Brigade during the war. A site in Forge Road had been leased from the Tredegar Estate since 1935 with a view to expansion, and it was here that the 'green hut', as it was known, was delivered in sections and erected for the Home Guard in 1940, adjacent to an old Nissen hut used by the National Fire Service.

The original Home Guard volunteers, 1940. From left to right, standing: Dave Willetts, Cyrus Hughes, Ken Harrington, Gwyn Watson, Eric Coleman, Vic Perkins, Ray Bristow, Albert Jenkins, G. Allsopp, Ron Beach, Vic Pearce, Fred Buckley, T. Williams, E. Williams, Percy Heath. Kneeling: Michael Cross, Gordon Sanders, Fred Phillips, Danny Dowdeswell, Bill ('Pandy') Richards, Albert Rodway, Don Powell, Reg Dowdeswell, Wilfred Harris.

Presentation of British Legion awards to several men including Messrs Moyle, Hawkins, Luke, Morgan, Watson, Phillips, Askey and Hartley.

Where there's a will

'Sorting through family papers when my uncle died, we discovered telegrams and letters which showed that his brother who was 18 years old had been very seriously wounded in France. The family were told that no one could visit him, although several more telegrams were received saying he was dangerously ill. Somehow my grandparents must have managed to get to him, because there was also a letter from his nurse saying he would soon be home, and his recovery was due to their visit.' [BW]

Comfort Fund

A village Services Comforts Fund was set up which operated through the Legion. This enabled postal orders and parcels of gloves, scarves, balaclavas and socks knitted locally to be sent to men and women serving at home and abroad. Those who had been honoured or mentioned in dispatches were given an inscribed Benson gold watch. Presentations were made at the Legion or in the 'Top Club'.

Most of the surplus in the Comforts Fund was set aside at the end of the war towards adding the names of those who had fallen to the War Memorial. The new inscription and names were unveiled by Col. J.D. Griffiths at a service held on 18 October 1947. The remainder was shared amongst all the men and women whose names were on the Comforts Fund list. Rector F.A. Oswell in July 1947 wrote of the gift 'though small in intrinsic value, yet it comes with our very best wishes for your future'.

Your country needs you

In the six years from 1939 to 1945, Machen saw many young men and women depart to theatres of war in Africa, Europe and the Far East. There were some families who had at least three children serving and families who were to suffer bereavement coupled with a double sense of loss when their loved ones were laid to rest in foreign fields. Many men were prisoners of war in Europe and the Far East, being held, in some cases, for as long as five years. Other servicemen and women would find themselves sent to places as far apart as the Phillipines and North Africa and occasionally meeting up with brothers, sisters, cousins and friends en route in Singapore, Cairo and Athens.

Like their fathers and grandfathers before them, those who left Machen for service in the many and varied branches of the Army, Navy and Air Force are modest in recounting their experiences, feeling that they were all part of a national effort to defeat evil, and that everyone's job was vital whatever it was. Mindful of their wishes we mention but a few facts as a tribute to them all.

Many, leaving Machen in their late teens, did so for the first time. Holidays were by no means universal before 1939, and to go abroad was a pipe dream! Some youngsters joined the Territorials in August 1939 simply because it meant a chance to go to camp. Family ties were abruptly cut, and many were very homesick. Some men joined the ATC (Air Training Corps) and at 18 years of age found themselves volunteering as air crew members. This was to involve such operations as bomber raids over Germany which could mean flying for periods of five to nine hours, dependent on the target. It could be Hamburg, it could be the Czech border. The latter journey involved carrying as much as 2,000 gallons of fuel which had to be carefully monitored for a safe return. With the invention of radar, an essential task was the dropping of 'window', strips of aluminium foil, at intervals to disrupt the beams and so mislead the enemy in interpreting the size of the attacking force. Air crews in turn depended on the maintenance crews on the ground, and the personnel who plotted their course.

Those enlisting in the Army could find themselves, with an absolute minimum of training, in France, even on guard duty the night they arrived, with rifle but no ammunition. To hold a communication line in a French village completely alone for a week, and then to be told to get to the beaches at Dunkirk for evacuation the best way

Ruperra Castle as it was before its decline. Ruperra Castle was requisitioned after Dunkirk and Dutch troops were billeted there. A fire in December 1941 greatly damaged the building, injuring one Dutch soldier and three firemen. Indian and British troops were under canvas there. Some men married local girls, and remained in the area.

90

you could, must have been a nightmare. Those who were in the Middle East found that the British sense of fair play was so strong that it was the German prisoners who had most of the bread while they had to exist on bully beef and little else! There were, sadly, Machen men who were sent to combat in the jungles of the Far East, and to endure forced labour from which they were never to return.

The Royal Navy together with the Merchant Navy were services without which people at home would have starved. They guarded and conveyed the vital supplies of iron ore, grain, machines and food which were under constant attack from German U-boats. Machen had men in both. Former apprentices at the railway sheds at Machen and Caerphilly were valuable assets to the engine rooms of many ship.

Many Machen girls were also in the Services; most were stationed in this country but some were abroad. Those in Belgium and Holland helped civilians get back to some normality after the war. They could find themselves going into hospital to list the belongings of those killed which included collecting their name tags, but whatever their nationality they had to be accounted for, and families informed. Others joined the Land Army, and some worked in factories at Newport and Rogerstone making shells and wings for aircraft.

War in Europe ceased in May 1945, VE day being celebrated on 8 May. In Holland it was a soldier from Machen who typed documents relating to the surrender of the German Army arranged for two days later. He was locked into his office to avoid any outside contact while the documents were made ready for translation by the other Allied forces.

The Home Guard

Those who were too young or too old to serve did their bit as air-raid wardens, or in the Local Defence Volunteers later renamed by Winston Churchill as the Home Guard, which was attached to the 4th Battalion, Monmouthshire Regiment. The latter did parade practice by the 'ash tip' in Tyn-y-Waun field, and went for signalling instruction with John Coleman who had gained his experience in Salonika more than twenty years earlier.

'The first lot of guns we had were Canadian First World War Ross 303 Rifles, they had been in store for years, and were all packed in grease. After we had got them cleaned up, we were given a lecture on the parts of a rifle. "First thing", said Edwin Everson, our instructor, "make sure there is no bullet up the spout." He pressed the trigger, and a bullet went straight up into the ceiling! Then we had to go up to the tippers on the top of the mountain. That was to be the rifle range. Jack Haines, our policeman, was supposed to be training us. Well, we all fired at the target and hit it, he was the only one that missed!

At the crossing by the Traeth (Lower Machen) there was a slit trench which we had to guard. In the autumn of 1940 there was a big air-raid in Cardiff. We were in the trench and heard footsteps. Trevor Holland, my mate, said 'You go and challenge him, I will cover you'. I shouted 'Halt, who goes there?' No reply, the steps kept coming. I repeated it twice, and then loaded the magazine and shouted 'Halt, or I fire.' The figure looked up and I saw him just in time, it was Stan Buckley. He had been delivering a load of stone from the quarry, and the wardens had told him to pull in, leave the lorry and walk home. He was quite deaf and hadn't heard me.' [RD]

German parachutists on the mountain

'In 1940 I joined the Home Guard, and one night Cyrus Hughes and I were sent to patrol the mountain because a message had been received that enemy parachutists had been dropped at Pontllotyn and were making their way to Newport via the mountain. There we were, scared stiff, with one shot-gun and one cartridge between us which we were required to fire as a warning when we spotted the enemy. We heard movements and a cough. The enemy would appear at any moment it seemed, when out of the mist came a couple of sheep. Thinking back, one remembers an elderly visiting officer who solemnly told us amongst other gems, 'If a German comes into your shop, refuse to serve him and if you are not sure that he is a German, ask him to say Wendell Wilkie [an American politician]. If he is German, he will say Vendell Vilkie'.' [EJC]

The Black Out and ARP

Air Raid Precautions required all windows to be blacked out. This usually took the form of thick curtains or curtains lined with black material to keep any light from showing outside into the street which would help enemy aircraft. Air raid wardens would parade the streets, knocking doors if any lights did show. Street lights were not allowed, and people found difficulty in negotiating the several railway arches in the village. Buses and cars had their headlamps deflected downwards by means of a slatted metal disc, which made them look like glow-worms. Buckets of sand with a stirrup pump would be placed in front of buildings in the event of incendiary bombs being dropped, and everyone was issued with gas masks which were carried everywhere in cardboard boxes slung over the shoulder. Babies were to be put into a tent-like structure. Thankfully, these were never used.

Bombs (about 50 incendiaries) fell in Lower Machen near Machen House, in the woods near Penhow, on the chicken sheds at Cwm Nofydd and a 'stick' of bombs [250lbs] was dropped in the area round the Pymmer and the Gelli. None exploded, and they were defused by a bomb disposal unit which was stationed at the Gelli for several days.

Put that light out!

'My husband was an air raid warden section leader, and as the siren was next to our house it created such a noise that everything rattled on the dressing table. In spite of that, I'd have a terrible job to wake him up, and used to tell him the all-clear siren would be sounding before he was ready. 'Jim the post', as he was called, was also an air raid warden, and a real character. One night when the sirens went off, he was smoking and put the lighted cigarette in his pocket; 'I don't want the enemy to see the light', he said.' [KT] A warning of an air raid was given by the siren emitting a fluctuating wail; the all-clear signal was a steady tone.

'Mrs Bell was another village 'character'. She lived in a cottage by the old dram road, and when the sirens went off, she would run down to the side of the viaduct, and across the top screaming, 'The Germans are coming, the Germans are coming'. She was genuinely terrified.' [DW]

Food and clothing were rationed by means of coupons, and housewives had ingenious ways of making dried eggs [powdered and tinned] stretch when making cakes and other wholesome dishes. In those days gardening and allotments were an established way of life, and this was a great supplement to the family menu. Many kept a few chickens and possibly a pig. Some parts of the latter when slaughtered would be divided out with others who would return the favour when their animals were killed; home refrigeration was minimal, certainly no freezers!

Evacuees came to both Upper and Lower Machen, together with their teachers and were welcomed into local homes. In some cases mothers came with their children and lived on farms that had a spare room, looking after themselves. There remain a few who still keep in touch with their 'foster' homes, in the same way that friendships made in the services have been cemented by visits or cards being exchanged at Christmas.

VE and VJ days were celebrated in the village with street parties and singing. There was an air raid shelter in the grounds of the Church Room, and the piano was hauled out and put on top of this, and everyone sang their hearts out. George Keenan, with piano accordion, together with Mrs Askey and Mrs Bennett led the singing, and Mrs Phyllis Voyce who lived opposite the Church Room, had 'V for victory' lit up in lights in her front garden.

These were difficult years which were to have far reaching effects. Before the war there was not a great choice of employment, you usually followed whatever your parents did. After the war when many had seen other places, mixed with other nationalities, and when there were more job opportunities, social mobility was much easier. Women had taken over many jobs previously done by men, and had shown flexibility in running a home and doing an outside job. As one person put it, 'if it had not been for the carnage, it was an education', while another says, 'there seemed to be a wonderful sense of comradeship throughout the country'. A third said, 'My demob came in May 1946, and I returned with my wife to Machen, the village which I had missed so much and which has remained our home ever since. We turned out to be a lucky family, we three brothers returned safely. So many other families were never complete again.'

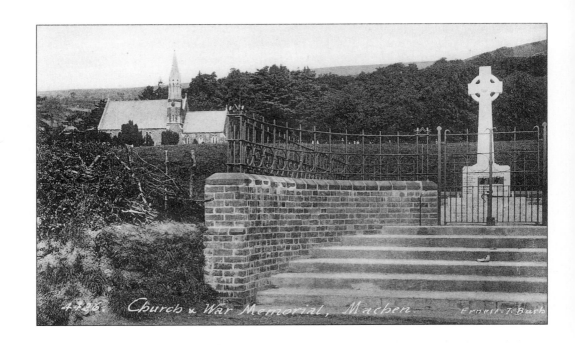

Church & War Memorial, Machen. Ernest T. Bush

War memorial

1914-1918

J. Banfield, W.E.C.A. Darby, L. Everson, W. Harrington, A. Harris,
J.H. Harris, P. Heath, H.J. Hoare, H. Hodges, A. Horton, W.T. Howells,
W. Jenkins, T.H. Johnson, R. Jones, J. Kew, F.G. Lewis, A. Matthews,
S. Mayberry, W. Morgan, J. Pugh, A. Rees, D.T. Rees, J.H. Richards, A. Rolls,
T. Rosser, W. Shute, A. Thomas, T.A. Thomas, H. Whittingham.

1939-1945

R.W. Beach, R. Credgington, M.C. Cross, C. Daley, D.J. Davies, R.G. Deverrine,
J.H.S. Evans, I.C. Green, H.J.L. Harris, A. Hill, F. Jeremiah, T. Jones MM,
L.C. Prince, W.S. Ransome, D. Rees, J.H. Rutter, C.F. Tuckwell, C.W. Whittles,
T.E. Worthington.

We will remember them

Eight
Village Miscellany

Lower Machen

The Forge cottages in the late 1890s. Many such buildings on the Tredegar Estate were renovated at the turn of the century. The old village had three public houses, The Rising Sun (now Forge cottages), The White Lion which stood opposite the old post office at what is now the entrance gates to Machen House), and The Bluebell Inn at the junction of the old main road with the Risca mountain road.

The beebole in the grounds of Machen House is listed in the National Monuments Record as late eighteenth or early nineteenth century. It is presumed to have been set into an older building or boundary wall being used as an apiary, or it could have been brought there to enhance the site. It is a rare example of this type of building. Roman artefacts have been found over the years in the vicinity, some as recently as 1996.

Draethen village, 1930. On the 'circuit' for walkers on Sunday evenings after worship, the tea shop run by Billy and Mabel Lewis was a popular stopping place. Behind these cottages was the 6 o'clock Field, venue for many chapel outdoor tea parties.

The Square, *c.* 1900. Situated in Church Street, there were thatched dwellings on the other side of the road adjacent to the old Post Office.

Upper Machen

Upper Machen or Ffwrrwm Uchaf started to grow during the 1850s expansion of industry. Chatham Row, Colliers Row, Green Row and New Row were all built at this time. The Llanarth Estate and the Wyndham Lewis Estate also owned ground in Machen, and part of Ysgubor Fawr farm was leased by them for building before the middle of the last century, hence the naming of Wyndham and Lewis streets. Lewis Street was also known as Clay Street, possibly because men living there worked in the ironworks or brickworks which required clay workers.

The old police station, 1906. PC Morgan is wearing a bush-style hat, a style which was replaced in 1914. The site is now occupied by a modern bungalow. Other dwellings which have disappeared were in the Dranllwyn and White Hart areas, and in the lane behind Russell House, a row of cottages known as Potters' Row. Several cottages at Cae Bach occupied by forge workers at the end of the last century have now been replaced by a small close, and three cottages on Quarry corner no longer exist.

The yard on Chapel Hill, said to have been adapted from farm buildings or cottages to stabling for the horses which pulled the drams up the Run. Also known as Twm Shon Howell buildings after the man who once lived there, and was the parish clerk. Today, the site is occupied by modern pensioners' bungalows, Bron-Rhiw.

The Crescent in the 1920s. The houses were the result of the 'No. 1 Building Club' of which Mr G.D. Inkin was the secretary, and cost £100 each. One of these was set aside during 1915 for a family of Belgian refugees at a rent of 8/- per week. Improved housing began around 1908 when a terrace of ten semi-detached homes was built opposite the recreation ground, followed by houses in Commercial Road and Forge Road. Sunnybank and Brynhyfryd were built by the council above the station and occupied by 1927. Pensioners' bungalows in the Crescent (1974) together with more council and private housing followed, including Graig View in 1955. The extensive Bovil site, after the demolition of the original house, is now occupied by many modern houses and bungalows. The total number of householders in Machen parish was 2,512 in 1991 with a population of 6,657 including Graig-y-Rhacca.

New Row

'My grandmother was born in Woodbine Terrace, near Green Row [no longer there], and when she married in 1900 she moved to New Row [230 people are recorded living there by this time]. The first house had a staircase in the kitchen, but by the time they got to the final house, No. 20, the interiors were far better shaped. Each house had a privy at the top of the garden. There were also several communal pig's-cots built in addition to the very important bakehouses which were also for shared use. I asked my Nan how she judged when the oven was ready, and was told on opening the door you put your arm in, and counted to a certain number. It was ten for loaf cakes, and seventeen for bread. There was a rota system whereby each house had a day or afternoon in which to bake. The water came from a well in the nearby woods, which was later connected to taps outside the houses until some time after the setting up of the Rhymney Valley Water Board in 1921.' [JW and TH]

Cleaning in Colliers Row

'Colliers Row [Riverside Terrace] was built for the colliers at the old pit. I used to help my aunt who lived there and had four of them to look after. The shed had a boiler with fire under, and I had to fetch water in buckets and fill the boiler to get hot water for their baths. There were four lots of clothes, sheets, Sunday best suits, and cleaning to do. I used to pack everything in tin boxes with paper in between each lot to separate each man's property.' [LR]

These houses were owned by the Tredegar Estate, and rents at the time of the Estate sale in 1920 varied from 10/- to 15/2 per month.

Wash day

'I began very early in the morning filling the wash-copper and lighting the fire underneath it. Few homes possessed hot water in those days. The clothes were first washed in a big tin bath using a rubbing board and the white articles boiled in the copper with a handful of suds and shredded yellow soap. For the final rinsing we used the blue bag which was also an effective remedy for wasp stings. Then came the starching of the required articles. All was ready now for the mangle, a huge iron contraption with wooden rollers. How turning the handle could make one's arms ache! When the clothes were dry, they were sprinkled with water, and rolled up ready for ironing. No electric iron came to our aid, our flat irons were heated on the fire, then rubbed on an emery board and wiped clean. [To tell when the iron was ready one had to spit on it]. This added more time and labour to our weekly wash.' [DD] Meyrick's shop had a large advertising poster stating 'Reckitts – out of the blue comes the whitest wash'].

Running hot water at last

'I was in my seventh heaven, when we moved into the Crescent in the late '30s because we had a copper. We used to light a fire underneath it, and the tap went from the boiler through the wall and into the bath. We had a bathroom, three bedrooms, three rooms downstairs and two elecric lights.' [KP]

Machen, early 1930s. Note 'tippers' on the mountain top, the spoil from Risca colliery, and Gadd's bungalow in the Vedw.

The Depression: blacklegs and soup kitchens

There were long strikes in the coalfield in 1921 and again in 1926, including the national General Strike after which came years of depression stoically endured by the people of the valleys. Machen was no exception, and there are memories still of strike-breakers known as 'blacklegs' being brought through Machen from Newport in cars with windows blocked up and police riding alongside. Men were without work for years, and women had to feed and clothe their families on very low benefits, supplementing the income by taking any cleaning, laundry or sewing work available, and the old school was used as a soup kitchen for the colliers. The keeping of an allotment was a vital part of the household economy.

Four-foot-long parsnips

'My father, Joe, was a fine gardener. He would dig down several feet for his onion bed. He had some onions, Good God Almighty, they weighed four or five pounds. One onion in an old-fashioned family frying-pan, and it was full to the top. We used to eat a lot of onions, us young kids, years ago. He used to have chicken manure, and we had an old-fashioned oven in the house; he'd put it in there on a tray, crush it up, dry it, put it on the table where we had our food, make it into a powder, and early in the morning he'd take it out to the allotment. He went to the Crystal Palace Show in 1921 with pansies, parsnips about four feet long, carrots and a rose that was grown on a blackcurrant tree. He grafted it, see, and that rose was black like velvet. He had six on this tree, and he won the gold medal. Because he was such a good gardener a well-known firm of seedsmen (Bees) asked him if they could have a sample of the soil from his garden. There was no flies on my old man so he went up to the Vedw and dug some earth from a mole tump and sent that to them.' [LJH]

Rabbit stew

'We always had a great big black steel saucepan that went on the hob on Monday for stew. It had to be huge because we were five children, seven in family altogether. A big black kettle was always kept on the side of the hob, the knob was cleaned with "Brasso". We used to eat a lot of rabbits, and you could get a bucket full of apples for one penny.' [KP]

Coal from the tips, from trains, from the wood

'I remember my father telling me we were in the middle of the Depression. He was unemployed and getting fuel from foraging in the tips on Machen mountain, one of many men, women and children out there, very often in bitter cold weather, some of the boys clad only in shirts, trousers and shoes.' [MH]

'My father told me that the woods would be alight with candles in jars which men took with them when they went into the wood to dig for coal. The local policeman was content with this state of affairs so long as his own coal shed was kept topped up, but one night a stranger on the beat came along. Hearing several men digging, he shouted to them 'Who's down there?' Back came the reply, 'Wocko, Dooko, Jacko' which understandably exasperated him, but those were their nicknames, and there wasn't much he could do about it. Dad said things became so desperate that he and several others would mount the coal train as it came round a corner from Bedwas colliery and shovel off as much as they could as it traversed the bend. There were others below who would bag and hide it. He felt the injustice very keenly, and in later years he took me to a spot in the woods near Penhow and said 'This is where the coal rises. If you are ever on hard times, dig here.' It sounds laughable now, but he was deadly serious. During the war bombs were dropped in that self-same spot in the woods and his fury knew no bounds. 'The buggers had my coal hole', he exploded.' [JW]

A view from the Gelli of the new pit which was never worked, 1930.

The first council bus service commenced in January 1922 running between Caerphilly and the Royal Oak, to be followed by the first Workmen's service in 1923. In July 1922 T. Beavis of Risca, had introduced a service from Newport to Machen which connected with the Bedwas and Machen UDC (Urban District Council) services, as above.

Beavis' service was passed on to the Dan-y-Graig Bus Company which ran from Newport to the Conker Tree, eventually being taken over by the Western Welsh Bus Company in 1936.

Electricity for the first time

The coming of electricity in 1925 in addition to providing light opened up the world of broadcasting, although some houses already had home-made sets. Enterprising enthusiasts would go up the mountain to 'where the Devil broke his apron strings' and collect white quartz crystals to make their sets. Gas came much later which has enabled choice in central heating and other household appliances. The traditional coal fire which was prominent in all homes at the beginning of the century, especially since colliers were allowed a ton of coal every month, is now the exception rather than the norm. The latest houses built in the village have no chimneys.

Home-made radios

'I think Bert Sydenham was the first one to make a proper wireless [as radio was then known], and my father was the second. It was complete with valves, transformers, condensers, big high tension battery and an accumulator. This had to be taken periodically to Jesse Owens in Commercial Road to be charged. We used to listen with headphones, but only one person at a time. By putting the headphones astride a large biscuit tin you had a primitive loudspeaker. It required an aerial attached to a post as high as a rugby goal post.' [CC] Such is the advance of modern communication that there is now a TV relay mast on Machen mountain, sited on the spot where a ceremonial bonfire was lit to celebrate the relief of Mafeking in the Boer War, and for the coronation of Edward VII. Speed's map of 1610 and a Manorial survey dated 1630 indicate that a beacon was maintained here for lighting if danger threatened.

A wheelbarrow robbery

'Many houses did not have a back entrance, and the coal was left in the road outside the houses. My father, who worked on the railway, had made a large wooden wheelbarrow which was often borrowed by miner neighbours to barrow the coal through their houses to the coal store. It was always returned full as a token of thanks. It was stolen once when the Co-op was burgled. The thief put a safe in it, and it was found in the Harrow Seeding [a field beyond the Pandy]. Dad was ticked off by the policeman for leaving it outside.' [EJC]

Machen Stars RFC, 1908-9 season. Back row: W.H. Davies, O. Hicks, W. Davies, G. Burton, L. Everson, J. Hicks, T.J. Harrington (secretary), A. Willetts, F. Humphris (treasurer). Middle row: W. Harper, W. Beeston, E. Davies, W. H. Sheppard, C. Saunders, E. Jones, S. Thomas, R. Howells (trainer). Front row: J. Jones, R. Escott (captain), G. Rogers.

Machen RFC

Machen Rugby Club commenced in 1871, and was a founder member of the Welsh Rugby Union (WRU) when it was formed in 1881. Its shield is among those proudly displayed at the Arms Park headquarters. Machen also had teams named the Stars and the Greys which were playing before 1900. It produced many fine players, F. Purdon capped between 1881 and 1883, Mel Rosser in 1924 and W.A. Everson, 1926 who all started their playing careers in Machen. The most successful player was probably Malcolm Thomas who captained Newport, various services' teams and Wales. He toured with the British Lions in 1950 and 1959, gained 27 Welsh caps, and scored the winning try in Ireland to secure the Triple Crown for Wales in 1950. A schoolboy cap was awarded to Arthur ('Puss') Minty direct from Machen School, and in the early 1960s three Machen boys John ('Nino') Berni, Godfrey Davies, and Hugh Hague gained caps at secondary school level. The latter was only 17 years old when he died being struck by lightning when sheltering from a storm. Another name forever associated with the club as player and official was Jack ('Shon') Davies. To many 'Shon' was Machen Rugby Club. He served on the Welsh Rugby Union Committee for thirteen years, and was the first retiring committee member to be presented with an inscribed silver salver.

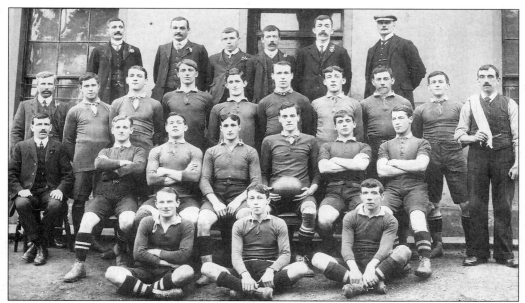

Machen RFC, 1911-12 season. Back row: J. Potter, J. Kellow, T. Richards, J. Moses, W. Minty, T. Mallett. Second row: D. Stephens, D. Stephens, D. Thomas, G. Harris, J. Hicks, W. Jones, M. Anthony, E. Buckley, S. Thomas, J. Moses (trainer). Third row: M. Moses (hon. secretary), A. Davies, W. Roberts, R. Escott, F. Jones (captain), S. Jenkins, W. Beeston. Front row: G. Rogers, C. Hodges, W. Moses.

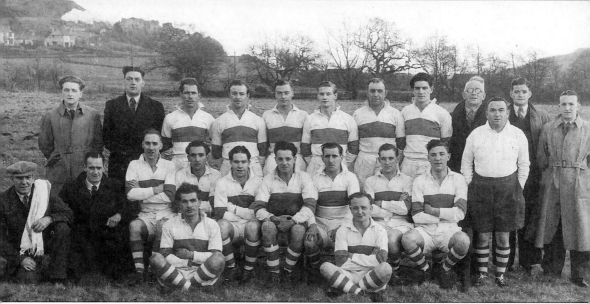

Machen RFC, 1948-49 season. Back row: K. Harrington. R. Davies, D. Gooding, D. Powell, R. Carter, M. Lewis, F. Emms, M. Bennett, David Jones (WRU), J. Watkins. Middle row: C. Everson (trainer), Jack Davies (hon. secretary), G. Mobley, B. Rowlands, K. Hicks, D. Hartley (captain), L. Hill (vice-captain), D. Spargo, M. Everson, C. Gregory (referee), M. Thomas. Front row: R. Gooding, R. Harris. Note the steam-train coming around lime-kiln corner.

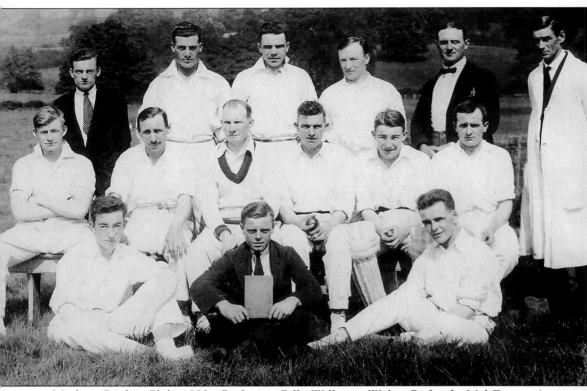

Machen Cricket Club, 1920s. Back row: Billy Williams, Walter Richards, Mel Davey, Artie Harrington, Harry Wilde, Bert Beeston. Middle row: Tommy Young, Jaffa Thomas, Fred Jones, Dil Davey, Basil Jones, Bryn Richards. Front row: Ken Harrington, Tal Buckley, Wally Williams.

Machen Cricket Club

Machen Cricket Club celebrated its centenary in 1978, but cricket was being played here before 1878, the home ground being in Lower Machen. Use of the pitch was originally granted by Mr F. Stratton of Machen Plas, free of charge. Before the First World War four members of the Stratton family played for the club. Along with Sir Leolin Forestier Walker and D.A. Ewing, an ex-Yorkshire cricketer, two of the Strattons were selected to play for Monmouthshire. Between the wars, the older and later members maintained the strong tradition and continued improving not only the club's reputation, but also its facilities. Up until 1934 teas were provided in the village schoolroom, but then a new pavilion was erected which provided changing-rooms and a team-room at the field. Ken Harrington was one of the prime movers in this connection. In this later period both Malcolm Thomas and Dilwyn Evans were selected to play for the Welsh Secondary Schools. Machen Cricket Club still plays at Lower Machen as a member of the newly introduced league structure. At the end of the Second World War, dedicated volunteers, after several years of hard work, re-established the ground together with improved facilities, in addition to the pavilion erected in 1934.

Machen Baseball Club, 1921. Back row: Ron Stephens, V. Whittingham, W. Harris, George Burton (chairman), A. Emery (umpire), R. Thomas (vice-chairman). Second row: T. Maddocks (trainer), J. Hicks (hon. secretary), Ivor Harris, J. Jones, F. Richards, J.E. Everson, T. Rees, T. Rosser (treasurer), A. Waters (committee). Third row: A. Bodrell, W. Jones, Mel Everson (captain), W. Whittingham, T. Young. Front Row: S.V. Fairfax, Mascot, H. Voyce.

Baseball in Machen

Welsh baseball commenced in 1892 with international matches between Wales and England first being played in 1908. John ('Emmy') Everson, was the first secretary of Machen Baseball Club in 1920. Many of us grew up with baseball 'down the rec' and remember the opposing teams from Newport and Cardiff, Pill Harriers in particular. When Machen won the league or the 'cup' it was filled up with lemonade for the 'kids' to have a sip. One of the players capped for Wales was Ralph ('Rajah') Morgan, who was also acclaimed for his achievements in rugby.

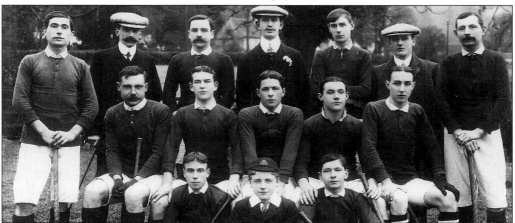

By 1907 there was a male hockey team in the village. Bert Beeston was captain, and the 1913-14 fixture list shows the team playing matches at Cardiff, Newport, Pontypridd, Barry, and Llanishen weekly during the season. Joe Morgan (father of Ralph), was a team member, together with E.W. Phillips, J. Davies, D.C. Price and F. Lewis.

Myrtle Wade (*née* Thomas) was capped for Wales at hockey against England in 1950. This is fixed in the minds of of us because she was capped the same day as brother Malcolm played for Wales in the Triple Crown victory mentioned on p. 104. She also represented Wales in matches against Scotland, Ireland and Holland the same year before retiring. Malcolm retired from the sport in 1959 after touring with the British Lions to New Zealand. Their grandfather, Aaron Skuse, had played for the Machen Old Greys rugby team before emigrating to America.

Machen Table Tennis Club, Newport League Division 4 Champions, 1956-57. Their playing headquarters were at the Machen British Legion (Nissen hut). From left to right: J. Brussalis, J. Evans, A. Rogers (captain), R. Beavis, B. Bateman, C. Voyce, B. Rees. Previously played on a friendly basis in the Co-op basement, the game really 'took off' in 1932 via the Church Youth Club. Successfully revived after the war by the Rev. F. Secombe, it led to the formation of the Newport Church Table Tennis League in 1950, Machen being the first champions. The senior club, formed in 1954, was affiliated to the Table Tennis Association of Wales, competing in the very strong Newport League and winning many awards.

Mr Ron Davies MP at Machen Bowling Club opening day on 7 June 1992. Formed in 1985, this is the most recent addition to the Machen sporting scene. It has already built up a good reputation, playing matches at home and away with many longer-established clubs.

An early soccer team outside the Tredegar Arms. Although played in the early days it never really became a permanent part of the sports scene. In the 1920s a team played down by the old forge, on a field known as the Pound, but it was not until 1959-60 that the game was revived with the introduction of a youth team which won honours in the Newport and Monmouthshire leagues, touring Germany as league champions representing Newport. The Pound was also the venue for the Machen boxer, Jack Newton, who trained in a barn there with his sparring partners, including Terence Davies.

Machen School football team, 1925-26. Back row: Mr Emrys Llewellyn, Stan Green, 'Fly' Baynton, Garfield Vaisey, Mr G. Inkin, Harry Broomfield, Noel Harris, Mr J.T. Spinks. Second row: Lyn Harding, Ron Fitzgerald, Colston Buckley, Dai Willetts, Arthur 'Aggar' Davies, Reg Hicks. Front row: Arthur 'Clem' Thomas, Ron Ellis, Alban Davies, Garfield Shepherd. One game still remembered was against a team of Basque refugees at the time of the Spanish Civil War (1937). The magnet for soccer in the district was the Trethomas Bluebirds, which attracted players from Bedwas and Machen.

The Top Road Harriers, 1922. From left to right, back row: T. Holland, W. Rogers, L. Jones. L. Shepherd, L. Thomas, W. Price, A. Rogers, R. Thomas. Front row: G. Shepherd, H. Bloomfield, S. Rogers, W. Salathiel, B. Jones, D. Mayberry, J. Williams.

Childhood gangs and games

'Boys had their own "gangs". We had the Top Road Harriers in 1923 which played football and cricket against other lads. There were also Chatham, White Hart, Crescent, Top Road and Napier Street gangs. I was too young to join, but followed them faithfully. My greatest plaything was my hoop and guider which I bowled round the lanes and up the paths. We would run miles, two or three of us. I had more fun with my hoops than any other game at all.' [AR]

'One of my earliest memories was in infant school. There was a long iron handle which was used to hold back the big gate. We used to put it down inside our collar, and it became a petrol pump like the one opposite school where Mr Gadd sold ROP (Russian Optima Petrol) petrol. After filling up, we would run round the playground, changing gear with accompanying revving and speeding sounds. Imagination did the rest.' [EJC]

'We played rap tap ginger, bambarino or strong horses and weak donkeys, and went on paper chases. The best runner carried the paper in an *Argus* bag, and there would be about ten following him. Up past the quarry, through the Park wood, down to Rhiwderin, finishing up around Rhyd-y-gwern and home. Great for cold winter nights.' [RD]

'Hopscotch was a favourite game. We drew patterns all over the road and played there, and we would tie a rope from the gate across the road, and skip. Can you imagine trying to do that today? Another thing we would do was to climb the mountain and pick wimberries for mother to make tart. One day I had picked a lovely lot and coming down over the stile I tipped them, oh, I did cry.' [DV]

'There were wooden-wheeled scooters, later light metal ones, tricycles, all sized box cars, very home-made, footed by discarded pram wheels, plain board flyers, narrow with little pulley-wheels that dug into the ground rope-steered and heel-propelled, pogo sticks and spindly stilts, but no bikes.' [1914, LS]

The pictures

'The cinema age brought a new dimension to everyone's lives. There was a special morning showing every Saturday at Bedwas Hall for children, and in the early days of silent films, the dialogue was flashed on the screen where necessary, while the piano provided the necessary accompaniment which alternated dependent on the action. We boys would copy Hopalong Cassidy's exploits, and swagger out of the hall drawing our guns at the least excuse. Our neighbour's grandmother, 'Granny Davies' who was in her seventies, often used to come with us, and she would be more excited than we were. She would jump up brandishing her umbrella and shout 'Look out, look out, he's behind you.' [EJC]

'My grandfather could read, so he often had to sit in the middle of the row in order to read to the others each side of him.' [JW]

'I remember my gang went round with Z engraved on their foreheads after watching *The Mark of Zorro* with Tyrone Power, and I also recall the routine perambulation of the attendant with the disinfectant gun which was mercilessly sprayed on us all.' [MB]

'Tredegar Estate always used to have a special day for paying the ground rents, and my grandfather and his friend went to Newport in their best suits to do this. Afterwards they thought they would go to the cinema to see what it was like. I don't know what the film was, but it was depicting stormy weather and rain. The one said to the other, 'We'd better go home, because we'll get very wet soon'.' [MI]

The Ffwrrwm Ishta inn the first half of this century. Fairs, with swings and roundabouts, were sometimes held here together with the occasional visit by a circus. Barnum and Bailey or Bostock's Menagerie would parade through the village en route to Newport.

Machen carnival possibly part of the celebrations for the coronation of George V in 1911. Ebrill Edwards, postmaster is shown on the box seat, Cornelius Roberts formerly of Ty Canol but then landlord of the Ffwrrwm Ishta in tweeds and cap, bowler-hatted Griffith Inkin, headmaster of the school, and Mat Matthews, coachman.

On the same occasion in 1911, Grace Smith of The Barracks is pictured with a decorated bicycle, one of the many that her father hired out by the day.

Machen carnival in 1952 showing Mr Harold J. Finch MP crowning the carnival queen, Dorothy Chilcott. Her attendants were Kathleen Panting, Gwyneth Hutchings, Ann Dowdeswell and Kevin Taylor. The float was decorated by Mrs Walley.

Machen Carnival

'We had marvellous carnivals with jazz bands and fancy dress parades. On May Day in the '30s the children would dance round the maypole. Mrs Vodden and Mrs 'Provy' [Providence] Morgan would make beautiful costumes and decorate floats. One year the children were dressed in different coloured crêpe paper costumes to depict sweet peas, on another occasion they held branches and were dressed as fairies to depict a fairy glen.' [KP]

WI carnival float. From left to right: Mrs C. Bundy, Mrs M. Brown, Mrs M. Wollan, Mrs M. Hicks, Mrs L. Askey.

Organ grinder

'My father, Alfred Cage, was Secretary to the Machen Nursing Assocation in the '30s. for which he organised carnivals and jazz band competitions. Together with Ritchie Rees and Ivor Llewellyn he walked miles with a barrel organ to make money for the fund. First of all they had a monkey, but alas, it had to go when it bit Ivor. As a result of their efforts we had Nurse Jenkins as our village nurse for many years.' [BR]

Machen Gymnastic Club was originally the Church Boys' Gymnastic Club started by Mr J.H. Hufton, assisted by his son, Doug, in the early 1930s. It attracted boys from 7 to 14 years, and later recruited girls and young adults. The gym club gave annual displays and was greatly helped by the gift of equipment including parallel bars and vaulting horse which the leaders were invited to select from Lord Tredegar's private gymnasium at Tredegar House. Many of their activities were accompanied on the piano by Mr Leolin Anthony who was also one of the church organists.

British Legion branch and women's section annual dinner, 1955. Back row: Major V.D.H. Elkington, Mrs C. Caston, Mrs J. Everson, Mr F. Godel, Mrs B. Harris, Mr J. Everson, Mrs J.T. Spinks, Mr W.E. Knight. Front row: Mrs I. Thompson, Major Ifor Jones, Dame Regina Evans, Major J.T. Spinks, Mr G. Cook, Mrs E. Johnston. After the Second World War, the British Legion acquired both the huts on the Forge Road site, and the British Legion (Machen) Club and Institute was formed, in addition to the branch, in 1946. The buildings have been upgraded over the years with the additions of a concert hall, games room and skittle alley. Today it serves a dual role as a United Services Club and as a temporary surgery, pending building of a permanent medical centre. The branch has a very active women's section and continues to promote the welfare of ex-servicemen and women and their dependants.

First committee of the Machen Working Men's Constitutional Club in 1921. From left to right, back row: R.T. Richards, T. Maddocks, M. Sheppard, J. Phillips, J.H. Hicks, W. Williams, D.G. Stephens, P. Phillips. Front row: F. Whittingham, F. Haskins, M. Moses, J.S. Thomas, B. Hill. Early meetings were held in Sudeley House, Chapel Hill, then in an old Army hut by the Dranllwyn bus-stop of today. The club moved to its present site in 1956, the building being converted through the voluntary labour of members.

Gilbert and Sullivan Society, 1950s. The group includes: Messrs Oxford, Bundy, Jenkins, Johnson, Thomas, Lewis, Maddocks, Rev. F. Secombe. Drama and music were among the many social and cultural activities carried on. The Village Hall, opened in 1949 by Alderman T.J. Jones JP, and the old Church Room have provided venues for many successful productions of the Machen Dramatic Society, and the Gilbert and Sullivan Society.

Machen Dramatic Society's production of Ladies in Retirement. Back row: Bill Panting, Kathleen Panting, Donald Willis, Marjorie Williams, Mary Sharples, Fred Brown, Victor Drake. Front row: Richard Willis, Megan Baynton, Beryl Drake, Rae Bull, Eva Stephens, Mrs N. Willis, Stella Spinks. The stage set was made by Bill Panting.

Mr Morley's Mixed Choir, post-Second World War. From left to right, back row: Tudor Hayward, Ted Phillips, Alf Walley, Hubert Thomas, Fred Brown, Graham Beeston, Tom Rees, Victor Matthews, Reg Rees, Lloyd Harris, Bernal Rodway, Walter Harper. Second row: Mrs Novello Bennett, Mrs Edith Hayward, Mrs Enid Harrington, Mrs Jack Harris, Mrs Edmunds, Mrs Oliver Burnett, Mrs Mabel Williams, Mrs Alma Harper, Mrs Coral Coleman, Mrs Gwen Matthews. Front row: Mrs Alice Davies, Miss Betty Harris, Mrs Violet Harper, Miss Eleanor Williams, Mr Jack Morley (conductor), Rev. F.A. Oswell, Mrs Wollan, Mrs Victor Matthews, Dorothy Wintle.

Mr Ebrill Edwards and his Male Voice Choir in Tyn-y-Waun field, pre-First World War. His bardic name was Gwilym Lon.

The choirs of Mr Edwards and Mr Morley

Mr Ebrill Edwards, the postmaster at Upper Machen, was also organist at St Michael's, Lower Machen, and a meticulous conductor for several decades up to the 1930s. At Upper Machen, Mr J. Morley was conductor at St John's and also conducted choirs comprising members of other chapels, carrying on into the 1940s and '50s.

'On one occasion Mr Edwards had a mixed choir and we were to sing And Grant a leader, Brave and Bold in the local eisteddfod which was held in Mr Llewellyn's field at the back of the Ffwrrwm. We rehearsed, and he stopped us and said, 'There's two ladies got to go from here'. What he meant was that instead of singing 'and grant'... 'and bold', we were not sounding the 'ds'. It sounded like Ann Grant and Ann Bold. He was very particular. I was also in Mr Morley's choir when we competed at Cwmfelinfach. We made sure we got there in time by walking over the mountain and went on the stage at midnight. We won first prize with a song called The sea has its pearls. We came home by bus, and they were waiting in the street to see how we got on. We all got out, stood there and sang it all over again.' [IR]

Members of the Horton family wind group. From left to right, back row: William, Albert and Ernest. Middle row: Mary Jane and William Henry. Front row: Alfred, Stanley and Ivor.

Two members of the Woodruff family from the Vedw House out for a spin in their Morgan run-about, one of the earliest of several that they owned.

Charabanc outing from The Tradesmans Arms to Coney Beach, Porthcawl. Among those pictured are Dai Hughes and Bill John.

British Legion outing to Lingen Hall, Herefordshire, by invitation of Sir Alfred and Lady Nicholas. Sir Alfred was president of the Machen branch, from 1960 to 1973, and patron from 1974 to 1984. Lady Ethel was women's section president from 1967 until 1977. The Nicholases were generous benefactors to many aspects of Machen life.

Sir Alfred and Lady Nicholas at Buckingham Palace on the occasion of his knighthood.

Church Street, early this century. Ffwrrwm Ishta is in the centre background.

Machen Touring Club visit to Blackpool in 1906. From left to right, back row: Herbert Harper, Bill Haskins, Tom Hicks, -?-, George Phillips ('Bodger'), Edwin ('Edmund') Rowlands, Mark Anthony, -?-, Sam Willetts. Front row:? Moses, Alderman Tom Jones ('Tommy Mount'), Tom Hughes ('Lamp Lighter'), Benjamin ('Beniah') Jones.

Machen outing to Blackpool half a century later. The group includes Harold Harris, Herbert White, Ann White, Jean White, Nancy White, Tom Rees, Mrs Jenkins, Mrs I. Jenkins, Mrs J. Harris, Mrs Maggie Davies (Bedwas), Hazel Horton, Mrs Rees, Mrs Connie Jones, Mr Bert Jones, Mrs Annie Jones, Mrs Gadd, Mrs Reg Young, Mrs M. Davies, Mr Davies, Mrs Williams, Mrs Amy Rosser, Mrs Doris Edmunds, Ithel Jenkins, Mavis Jones, Mr L. Davies.

Prize ticket awarded to Kathleen Jones at the sports held to celebrate the coronation of King George VI and Queen Elizabeth on 12 May 1937.

Silver Jubilee celebrations 1977 at Wyndham Street.

Machen, immediately post-war. Note the pre-fabs, the sites of which were later offered for private development, sitting tenants being given first refusal.

Christmas magic from the 1950s showing the sleigh provided by Sir Alfred Nicholas which visited Machen for many years distributing bags of sweet and oranges to excited youngsters.

The arrival of the family car, television, video, Walkmans and cheap package holidays abroad are all major sources of entertainment and have led to the decline of many 'more communal' village activities. The public houses that remain operate now under less strict licensing laws and are still popular, but as much nowadays for eating out as for drinking. However, The Rising Sun near the Gelli, The Crown in Llanarth Street, The Tredegar Arms, and Lewis's Hotel at the top of Church Street, popularly called the 'glue pot', are now private homes. The Good Companions, the Over 50s Club, the Village Produce Association, (now the Gardening Club) Machen & Sautron Twinning Association, the Probus and Rotary clubs are organisations which have come about since the 1950s. The Village Produce Association played host to *Gardeners Question Time* in 1961 when the BBC recording van visited the village. A most popular and valued addition has been the library which opened in 1988.

Machen from the east in the 1970s. The market garden of Tyn-y-Waun is now being developed for housing.

Epilogue

We bring this journey through the past to a close with three quotes from the fund of reminiscences we have been privileged to record:

'There was tremendous respect given to people years ago.'
'Well, when I look back, it's like a dream.'
'What a simple lovely life we had, didn't we? We had to make our own fun.'

Change, however, is ongoing and inevitable.

Sources and further reading

Newport Reference Library (South Wales Argus and other local papers; trade directories; census returns, maps, letters of David Jones (Ref. q. MOOO 012 JON), electoral registers); Gwent Record Office (Minutes of First World War Comfort Fund (Ref. D. 304. 0049); Minutes of First World War Belgian Refugee Fund (Ref D. 314. 0046); Correspondence re: Machen schools; Machen tithe map; Baptist records; Glamorgan Record Office; National Industrial and Maritime Museum; Church of England Record Centre; National Library of Wales – Tredegar Estate records; Machen School log books; Machen church records; Diaries of W. Beechey and P.T. Woodruff; The Welsh Office, Maps department; Machen Cricket Club, centenary booklet.

D.S.M. Barrie (revised by R.W. Kidner), *The Brecon and Merthyr Railway*.
G. Beeston, *Bedwas and Machen, Past and Present*.
A. Byles, *History of the Monmouthshire Railway and Canal Co.*
A. Clark, *The Story of Monmouthshire*.
E.T. Davies, *Monmouthshire Schools and Education to 1870*.
J. Davies, *The Chartist Movement in Monmouthshire*.
M. Hale, *Steam in South Wales* Vol 5.
Arthur Jones, *His Lordship's Obedient Servant and Dear Garf*.
Brynmor P. Jones, *Sowing Beside all Waters*.
Glyndwr G. Jones, *Chronicl Caerffili*.
M.G. Jones, *The Charity School Movement*.
R. Phillips, Tredegar, *The History of an Agricultural Estate*.
J.A.F. Pickford, *Between Mountain and Marsh*.
W. Rees, *Industry before the Industrial Revolution*.
H.P. Richards, *History of Caerphilly*.
Wesleyan Methodist Magazines.
Stewart Williams (ed.) *Vintage Buses & Trams in South Wales*.
I. Wright, *Branch Line Byways*.

Acknowledgements

The committee of Machen Remembered acknowledge with gratitude all the assistance they have received from so many people of the village, local and more distant. We thank them for the patience, courtesy, time and thought they have given to our enquiries, and for the wealth of archive material they have helped us to acquire. We also wish to pay tribute to Messrs Lloyd Davies [LD], Glyndwr Jones, and Bernard Smith whose photographic expertise has been so willingly given. Throughout the book the source of a quote or memory has been indicated using a code based on the individual's initials. The full names can be found below.

Mr and Mrs J.P. Adams, Mrs P. Adams, Mrs D. Bartlemore [DB], Miss M. Beeston, Mr M. Bennett [MB], Miss L. Bissett [LB], Mrs M. Carpanini, Mr and Mrs G. Carter, Mr R.M. Casserley, Mr D.C. Coleman [CC], Mr D.K. Coleman [KC], Cray Valley Ltd (Mr M. Jones and Mr W. Barge), Dr and Mrs J. Davies, Mrs A. Denty [ID], Mr R. Dowdeswell [RD], the late Mrs D. Driscoll, Mr J. Edwards, Mr B. Evans, Mr H. Everson [HE], the late Mr S. Green [SG], Mrs D. Griffin [DG], Mr Michael Hale, Mr L. Harris [LH], Mr M. Harris [MH], Mr R. Harris [RH], Mr T. Harris [TH], Mr W. Harris [WH], Mr D. Hartley [DH], Mr J. Hicks [JH], the late Mr L. Hill [LJH], Mrs V. Hopkins [VR], Mr D. Hufton, Miss L. Hunter (Machen Junior School), Mrs J. Isaacs [MI], Mr T. James [TJ], Mr and Mrs N. Jeremiah, Mr and Mrs R. John [RJ], Mr Alan Jones, Mr A.H. Jones [AJ], Mr and Mrs H. Jones, Miss M. Jones [MJ], the late Mrs M.M. Jones [MMJ], Mr R.W. Kidner, Mr G. Kingdon, Lens of Sutton, Mrs R. Lovell, Mrs S. Morgan, Mr D. Nicholas, The Oakwood Press, Mrs B. Onions, Mrs F. Partridge, Mr and Mrs D. Phillips [EP], Mrs E. Phillips [BP], Mrs E. Pugh, Mrs I. Rees [IR], Mrs B. Rogers [BR], Miss E. Rogers, Mrs M. Rogers [MR], Mr P. Rowlands, Mrs D. Rowles, Mrs L. Rymer [LR], the late Mr L. Salathiel [LS], Mrs H. Short, Mr and Mrs H. Spring, Mr B. Stephens, Mr J. Sweetland, Mr and Mrs J. Tamplin [JT], Mrs K. Thomas [KT], Mrs I. Thompson, Mr J. Turner, Mrs D. Vines [DV], Mrs P. Voyce, Mrs M. Wade [MW], Mrs J. Wakeley [JW], Mrs B. Walton [BW], Rev. C. Warren, Mr E. Watkins [EW], Mr G. Westcott, Mrs M. Williams, Mrs O. Williams, Mrs P. Woodruff, Mrs M. Woosnam, Mrs D. Wright, Mr Ian Wright.

We also wish to record the very great assistance given to us by Mrs Mary Tiffin and her staff at the Bedwas Centre whose support, encouragement and advice has been invaluable in establishing Machen Remembered, and our appreciation to the Chalford Publishing Company and Simon Eckley for undertaking the publication of this book.

Our sincere apologies if anyone has been inadvertently omitted.
We thank you all.

The Machen Remembered Committee:
Mr E.J. Coleman [EJC], Mrs D. Coleman [DC], Miss V. Cole, Mrs D. Gough,
Mrs K. Panting [KP], Mr A. Rogers [AR], Mr D. Spargo, Mr D. Thomas [DT],
Mrs D. Whitehead [DW].